Praise fo
The Jou

"Saying yes to God is not as easy as it sounds. When the initial excitement of fresh faith fades, hesitation and insecurity can delay the yes that we once offered so quickly. Brenda Palmer invites us into her story and skillfully shows us how to arrive at, or return to, our yes to God. If you want to truly understand how you can choose consistent obedience, you need this book."

—JADA EDWARDS, Bible teacher, speaker, and author
of *A New Way to Love Your Neighbor*

"My journey to where I am today is the direct result of the yeses I've given to God—especially the hard ones. Brenda Palmer offers a compelling and practical guide to embracing your own yes, unlocking the abundant, transformative path God has for you."

—TOURÉ ROBERTS, bestselling author,
businessman, and pastor

"*The Journey of Yes* is a beautiful blend of depth, honesty, and Spirit-led wisdom. Brenda Palmer writes like one who has wrestled with God and come out marked by grace. Her words invite you to stop resisting and start trusting, even when the path ahead is unclear. This book will stir your faith, steady your feet, and help you say your own courageous yes."

—CASSANDRA SPEER, bestselling author, Bible teacher,
host of the *Hard & Holy* podcast, and
vice president of Her True Worth

"Brenda Palmer's book is a powerful testimony that Christians can glean from at every age and stage of their faith journey. She takes us behind the scenes of her viral sermons and hit podcasts to show what it means to live a surrendered life. Palmer provides believers with a blueprint for saying yes to all God is asking them to do, even when they don't understand the way. This book is a must-read for anyone who is ready to deepen their relationship with God."

—GIA PEPPERS, award-winning host and creator
of the *Healed Girl Era* podcast

"Nothing impacts the journey of your life more significantly than a perpetual yes to God, and *The Journey of Yes* is a practical and life-changing clinic on the power of radical obedience. Brenda Palmer delivers a heart-riveting manual to help you pursue the glorious unknowns behind every yes."

—PHILIP ANTHONY MITCHELL, lead pastor at 2819 Church

"Watching my dear friend Brenda 'BP' Palmer walk out her yes with Jesus has been nothing short of inspiring. At a time when I was searching for a deeper connection with Christ, Brenda became a guiding light in my life. This is a powerful testimony of what happens when you surrender to God's call and trust Him with the process. Her story will stir your spirit and remind you that obedience to God isn't always easy, but it's always worth it."

—CRYSTAL RENEE HAYSLETT, actor, producer, singer, and host
of the *Keep It Positive, Sweetie* podcast

The Journey of Yes

The Journey of Yes

The Everyday Adventure of
Radical Obedience

Brenda Palmer

WaterBrook

WaterBrook

An imprint of the Penguin Random House Christian Publishing Group,
a division of Penguin Random House LLC
1745 Broadway, New York, NY 10019
waterbrookmultnomah.com
penguinrandomhouse.com

A WaterBrook Trade Paperback Original

Trade Paperback ISBN 978-0-593-60197-6
Ebook ISBN 978-0-593-60198-3

The Cataloging-in-Publication Data is on file with the Library of Congress.

Printed in the United States of America on acid-free paper

1st Printing

BOOK TEAM: Production editor: Jocelyn Kiker • Managing editor: Julia Wallace • Production manager: Maggie Hart • Copy editor: Kayla Fenstermaker • Proofreaders: Debbie Anderson, Julia Henderson

Book design by Virginia Norey

For details on special quantity discounts for bulk purchases, contact specialmarketscms@penguinrandomhouse.com.

The authorized representative in the EU for product safety and compliance is Penguin Random House Ireland, Morrison Chambers, 32 Nassau Street, Dublin D02 YH68, Ireland. https://eu-contact.penguin.ie

To my incredible parents,
Leonard + Cathy.

Thank you for being my anchors through this wild journey. Mommy, your unwavering encouragement to follow the voice of God and pursue my passions has been my guiding light. Dad, your boundless cheer and steadfast support have been my rock.

Even when paths diverge or understanding falters, you both show up, ride with me, and stand by my side. Your love and dedication mean more to me than words can express.

This book is a testament to your belief in me and, more importantly, to God within me.

With all my love and gratitude,
Your baby girl, Brenda

Foreword

From the moment I met Brenda Palmer, I knew her life would tell a story unlike any other—a story of unwavering obedience to God, no matter the cost. Over the years, we have become more than friends; we are sisters. Our bond has been one of shared prayers, shared tears, and shared victories. And through it all, her journey has inspired me deeply.

The Journey of Yes is not just a book to inspire or instruct—it's a life lived out loud and a testimony of what it means to follow Jesus wholeheartedly. As Apostle Paul once said, "Follow my example, as I follow the example of Christ" (1 Corinthians 11:1, NIV). Brenda's life echoes this call. She embodies what it means to live a life surrendered to God, one marked by obedience, courage, and trust.

Each of us has moments when our faith is tested, moments that define whether we will choose faith over fear, obedience over convenience. What sets Brenda apart is that these moments have come for her time and time again, sometimes in rapid succession. While many people face such crossroads every few years, I have watched Brenda give God her yes repeatedly, back-to-back, often at great personal cost. Her life is a template of radical obedience, showing us what it looks like to say yes to God whenever, wherever, and whatever the cost.

This kind of obedience is not easy—it requires sacrifice. I have seen Brenda walk away from her dream job, her dream career, and even dream opportunities she once longed for. In those moments, she chose to trust God over her own plans. She said no to the things that once defined her, because her identity is rooted not in worldly achievements but in Christ. And in His perfect timing, God has brought greater blessings than she could have ever planned for herself.

Her journey reminds me of Romans 12:1:

Therefore I urge you, brothers and sisters, by the mercies of God, to present your bodies [dedicating all of yourselves, set apart] as a living sacrifice, holy and well-pleasing to God, which is your rational (logical, intelligent) act of worship. (AMP)

When our lives are fully surrendered to Him, they become an act of worship, a powerful testimony that points others to Jesus. Brenda's life is a testament to this truth.

As you read this book, I want to encourage you: Don't just read it to be inspired, and then return to the comforts of routine. Read it with an open heart, ready to be transformed. Let Brenda's story challenge you to make your own commitment to God, to say yes to Him no matter the cost. There will be warfare—because the enemy knows his influence ends when you live a life fully surrendered to God. When your life is for the audience of One, the enemy loses his grip on you.

Get ready for an adventure. Saying yes to God will take you beyond your plans, beyond your comfort, and into a life of purpose and abundance. Brenda's testimony proves that even in the midst of challenges, God's faithfulness always comes through.

So, open your heart, lean in, and get ready to be forever changed. *The Journey of Yes* is an invitation—not just to read but to live a life fully surrendered to God.

Stephanie Ike Okafor
Pastor | National Bestselling Author | Podcast Host

Contents

Foreword by Stephanie Ike Okafor   ix

Introduction—Welcome to the Journey   xv

Chapter 1—Is God Enough?   3

Chapter 2—Where Are We Going?   21

Chapter 3—The Cost   43

Chapter 4—When Yes Leads
            to the Unexpected   59

Chapter 5—Finding Confidence in Your Yes   73

Chapter 6—Trusting God in the Uncertainty   93

Chapter 7—Courage Beyond Fear   109

Chapter 8—At the Point of No   127

Chapter 9—Does the Journey Ever End?   147

Conclusion—The Ultimate Yes   167

Acknowledgments   173

Introduction

Welcome to the Journey

Eyes squeezed shut, heart racing wildly, I struggled to breathe, clinging to the rails on either side of me. My feet felt like they were anchored by heavy weights, making it nearly impossible to move. As I stood there contemplating what I was going to do, I heard a voice say, "You're not alone." I opened my eyes and saw my coach in the pool below. We locked eyes, and a rush of bravery pushed me forward on the diving board. With each step, I took a deep breath. Once I reached the end of the board, I bent my knees, jumped, and plunged into the water. I broke the surface and shouted, "Yes! I did it!" At this time, I was about six or seven, taking swimming lessons at summer camp, and had just reached the stage where I was moving from the low dive to the high dive. I was terrified. When I was a child, my imagination often magnified my fears. Even though I loved the water, could swim well, and knew I'd surface safely, I still struggled to say yes to the challenge.

Not until someone reminded me that I wasn't alone did I find the courage to take the leap. I realized I'd be diving into the care of my instructor, who was waiting for me in the water. All I had to do was say yes.

Can you remember the first time you said yes to the unknown, having no idea where the yes would lead? What did it feel like? What was holding you back? I'm sure you've faced a similar time when you had to defy every instinct that screamed "No!" You chose to push past your fears and doubts and say yes. Taking a leap of faith isn't always an easy feat.

Saying yes often means confronting the fears conjured by our imagination rather than the actual challenges. I frequently feel unprepared, but a shift occurs when I realize I'm not alone. When I saw my instructor waiting in the water, I knew I wasn't facing the unknown by myself. The same is true with God. He leads us into journeys that seem overwhelming, but He promises to be with us every step of the way. Jumping off that high dive planted a seed of courage in me, showing me that saying yes to the unknown was a crucial step in life.

I'm often asked, "How did you have the courage to pack up and move across the country to L.A. with no solid plan or job waiting?" Another question is, "How did I have the courage to say yes to forgiveness despite a devastating betrayal that almost caused me to end my life?" The answer to both questions is that my faith led me beyond what I was afraid of to a life I couldn't have dreamed of. My fellowship with God led me on a journey that produced my yes. The answer was not ignoring the fear but recognizing that I had power over it and that all I really needed to do was just say yes.

Perhaps your first significant yes was not in swim class but maybe when you decided to pick up this book. It could have been in your decision to walk away from that toxic relationship and finally say yes to choosing you. Or maybe it was walking down the aisle to the altar and dedicating your life to following Jesus. Whether it's accepting a new job, moving to a new place, or starting a family, life is a journey of continually saying yes.

The journey of yes is both an invitation to do life with God and a continuous decision to follow Him. At its core, it represents the moment when we first respond to God's call, aligning ourselves with His purpose and design for our lives. This initial "yes" can be transformative—it sets us on a path of surrender and trust, opening our hearts to a new relationship with Him. But as we walk this path, we quickly realize that life is not a single act of obedience; it is a series of choices, each requiring us to say yes to God in fresh and profound ways.

Each step along this journey represents another opportunity to trust, grow, and deepen our dependence on Him. Some journeys of yes are monumental experiences of self-discovery or pivotal decisions that reshape our lives. Others are quieter, more subtle, challenging us not in what we gain but in who we become. Every act of saying yes draws us closer to the person God created us to be, revealing His character and His plans for us. At the same time, the journey of yes is also a singular, unified story—a lifelong adventure of faith and intimacy with Jesus. From the first "yes" that brought us to Him, to the countless decisions that sustain our walk, our lives tell the story of one great, ongoing journey with God. Whether it feels like the beginning of something new or the continuation of a well-worn path, the journey of yes invites us to live completely in God's plans, moment by moment and step by step.

I invite you to embark on the journey of yes—a deliberate, life-changing decision to walk in obedience to God in faith, surrender, and self-discovery. By saying yes to God, you open yourself to the person He has always known you to be—the person He lovingly created for His purpose. Each step is an opportunity to grow, trust, and deepen your relationship with Him. Wherever you are in your journey, I encourage you to take the next step, knowing that God's plans for you are filled with meaning, transformation, and boundless love.

I need to be up front—this path won't always be smooth. It will have its highs and lows, its occasions of stillness and its periods of turbulence. What I can assure you is that you won't be alone. Although this journey might feel like it's taking things from you or disrupting your life, with each yes, you'll come to see that the true purpose of the journey is to discover who God is, how He sees you, and who you will become as a result of your yes.

In my own journey, I find that before I give God my yes, I usually have a list of questions I want answered. I have a terrible habit of creating this world of hypotheticals inside my head that leads me into self-doubt, overthinking, and stagnation. That imaginary world makes a convincing case for the familiar always being the safest option.

I'm currently in the middle of giving God one of the boldest yeses I've ever had to give. This one feels different because I'm diving headfirst into the unknown. Not knowing the outcome of our yeses is what makes them hard to give. But instead of leaning into the world created by my fears, I've learned to access one rooted in my faith by using the Bible to create the foundation for my yes. Faith helps us overcome the fear of saying yes.

Fear is frequently the first emotion we experience when we receive a directive from God. But God's nature isn't to lead us into harm or danger. In reality, the true danger lies in ignoring His guidance and remaining stagnant. As we grow in our understanding of who God is, we come to realize that each instruction from Him brings us closer to Him, even if it doesn't always feel that way. This is where our faith comes into play. Both faith and fear demand belief: We can choose to trust the deceptions fear presents, or we can choose to believe in God's promises, even when their fulfillment isn't yet visible.

The easier decision will always be to go with what you know or what you are comfortable with. Most times we choose what is seemingly safe. But who told us that the easier option is always the best one? So many times along my journey, I've sided with fear, and let me tell you, it was not safe. Fear deceives us into accepting a false reality that where I am or what I'm currently doing is better than what God is asking me to do. Faith doesn't necessarily eliminate fear, but it helps us act despite it, providing the courage to move forward in uncertainty. Holding space for both fear and faith allows us to balance caution with hope, vulnerability with resilience, making us adaptable in the face of life's challenges.

No matter how fear has caused you to respond to God, by the end of this book I believe you will encounter Jesus in a way that you trust Him enough to say yes, despite how things may look. Here is a point of encouragement that levels me at the start of every journey: Just like the Lord commanded Joshua to be strong and courageous and not fear, we can have courage because of the promise that God will be with us wherever we go (Joshua 1:9). Even when we don't know where the yes is leading us, we can be confident that the One leading us will always be present. I'm excited to go on this journey with you and even bring along some of my friends.

Let's buckle up as we begin our journey of yes.

The Journey of Yes

1

Is God Enough?

One thing I have asked of the Lord, and that I will seek:
That I may dwell in the house of the Lord [in His presence]
   all the days of my life,
To gaze upon the beauty [the delightful loveliness and
   majestic grandeur] of the Lord
And to meditate in His temple.
—Psalm 27:4, AMP

Obedience and *surrender*—two words that can feel daunting. Interestingly, if you asked my friends to describe me, they'd likely say those words embody who I am. I take that as a compliment. One friend, Lami, often jokes that "Brenda's middle name is Obedience," and it's true; I've lost count of how many times I've approached them, saying, "I feel like God wants me to do [insert action here], so I'm going to try it."

I used to believe that the journey of obedience was all about saying yes to God so we can reach our goals, but I've come to understand that each yes allows me to peel back another layer of who God is. The journey of yes is the journey of drawing closer to God's heart.

Nike, one of my favorite brands, has the slogan "Just Do It," and that resonates with me. Sometimes I don't think twice;

I trust God's call and simply say yes. Other times saying yes is really tough, and the journey leads me into unexpected adventures, far beyond what I could imagine. Yet, through it all, I emerge as a better person, gaining a deeper understanding of God and a stronger desire to follow Him into the unknown.

The journey of yes is the journey of drawing closer to God's heart.

I wasn't your average child. As an eight-year-old, I admired Juanita Bynum, a powerful evangelist known for her boldness and prophetic calling. Even as a kid, I felt that God communicated with me in special ways. I'd have dreams and visions, and my love for Him was profound. My parents often took me to charismatic spaces, exposing me to the power of God, miracles, and healings at a young age. The Bible speaks about progressing from milk to meat (Hebrews 5:13–14), and even at eight, I sought a deeper relationship with God. I grew up in a traditional Baptist church, participating in the choir and junior usher board. Yet I always craved more. During this time of my life, my godmother would often visit an apostolic church that offered a different level of teaching, and she allowed me to tag along with her.

One Sunday, my mom visited the apostolic church with me. As the service neared its end, the pastor made an altar call to join the church. I looked at my mom and said, "It's time for us to join." Her eyes widened in disbelief; she worried about how my father would react. But I insisted that God was urging us to join that day. I took her hand, and we walked to the altar together.

As I think back, it's amusing how fearless I was. I understood that my dad wouldn't approve and that there were protocols for leaving a church, but none of that mattered. All I felt was a strong conviction that we needed to join. My mom listened to the voice of God in me, and we made that decision. A few months later, my dad followed suit, leaving our old church for the new one. Eventually, he even launched his own church.

That choice—offering a yes to God without thoroughly grasping its weight—created a ripple effect that transformed not only my life but also my parents' and many others' lives. If we hadn't taken that leap of faith, we would have remained stagnant, and my parents' calling might never have been realized. So many blessings stemmed from that decision to listen to God's voice.

So much of the journey of yes is embodied in a childlike trust in God, empowering us to simply say yes. This posture knows that, at a certain level, it doesn't matter what happens next, because the One asking us to say yes knows everything.

This journey of saying yes to God, however, isn't without its challenges. While taking those steps of faith can bring transformation and blessings, it also creates opportunities of deep reflection and self-discovery. Embracing a childlike faith means trusting without needing all the answers, yet sometimes God calls us to pause and examine the depths of our trust in Him.

When God asks me to follow Him into a new thing, He'll often ask me, "Can I be enough for you?"

When I first heard those words, I felt overwhelmed by a flood of emotions. Those six words were both a revelation about God's heart and an invitation to explore my own heart. *Is God enough for me?* That question served as a mirror, reflecting a hard truth: Despite saying yes to the Lord, I often found my devotion divided among other pursuits.

As humans, we naturally have big desires, and there's nothing wrong with that. The challenge arises when our longings for other things eclipse our desire for Him. In this instance of self-discovery regarding yet another journey of yes, I want to be transparent: I hadn't totally settled in my heart that God is enough. I know this may come as an unexpected and jarring confession, but I feel compelled to be real. As I asked myself this layered question, my heart's desires came to the forefront.

If I never get married, will God be enough for me?

If my parents go to heaven before I have children, will God be enough for me?

If I'm honest, I haven't yet reached a place in my life where I can say I wouldn't be knocked off my rocker if certain hopes and dreams don't come to pass. What I can say is that I'm on a journey with God that is so revealing of His nature and His unconditional love for me that it will eventually lead me to a place where I can give an unhindered yes. This is the journey God invites us all to.

Those six words mark both our starting line and our destination: "Can God be enough for you?" This question presents a spiritual crossroads we encounter repeatedly in life. God calls us to consider whether we can ultimately find satisfaction in Him alone. At the heart of saying yes to God lies the essential act of surrender. Not the lip service kind of surrender we often give, but one that says, "I surrender *all*." All my plans, will, emotions—everything I pursue in life—become secondary to my desire for God and what He desires for me. No matter the season of life we may find ourselves in, whether entering something new or making an exit, pursuing a next step or awaiting transition, the journey of yes is always rooted in the decision to relinquish our control.

Here is the truth of the matter: All the above is easier said than done. The decision to follow God's leading usually requires you to agree to something you can't see. That is the hard part. Most times there is no context for what you are being asked to do. We are basically required to recklessly let everything else go, and that can feel nearly impossible. The best thing about this is that we realize that we need someone to assist us in letting go. That is the surface need, but the truth of life is that in everything there is a need for God. We even need God to follow God.

The truth of life is that in everything there is a need for God. We even need God to follow God.

In Matthew, Jesus began to explain what life as His disciple requires, and He pointed us to the path of self-denial:

> Jesus told his disciples, "If anyone would come after me, let him deny himself and take up his cross and follow me. For whoever would save his life will lose it, but whoever loses his life for my sake will find it. For what will it profit a man if he gains the whole world and forfeits his soul? Or what shall a man give in return for his soul?" (16:24–26, ESV)

This scripture invites us to a heart posture of obedience. An often-hard truth to accept is that a surrendered life is really a life where we constantly die to our own desires.

We must die.

I don't mean physical death but the type of death that happens through submission and surrender. It's a posture that says, "I want God more than anything." The passage above can seem like a countercultural response to life. If we want life, we must lose it. We gain by giving up.

Even typing these things feels weird, like I'm not making sense. But in those words, we find the reality of the kingdom. To die is to gain. To lose is to win. Everything is upside down.

Jesus is our example. He gave up His life so that we could gain ours eternally. He modeled this method so that we can understand even while we are here on earth. If we lay down our life, we will pick up a life we never knew existed. We all have desires and plans. The journey of yes presents us with the opportunity to surrender those ambitions and expectations to Jesus and trust that the life He has for us is better. Even when we have no idea what His plans are.

Culture suggests that we should live our best life because we are going to live only once. Take advantage of every opportunity no matter what it costs. Seize the day. Live your best life. Just do you. I've been guilty of not only posting these as captions to my selfies but even adopting this deceptive ideology that my life is better in my own hands. Culture also conditions us to think that our life belongs to us. It doesn't. It was purchased with a price (1 Corinthians 6:19–20). Our God loved us so much that He sacrificed His beloved Son to ensure we could walk in fellowship with Him from the time we accept Him throughout eternity. For those of us who grew up in church, we've heard that truth so much that we can easily miss the magnitude of the gospel. Let's not do that. Our Savior, who is God, lowered Himself to walk this earth with us. He willingly sacrificed His life with the knowledge that not all of us would choose Him, yet He died for us all. No matter how undeserving we are, He saw us as worthy. Jesus thought we were to die for, and then He proved it. I know that a gift so precious and rare can be hard to fathom, but it's important that we understand the weight of the ultimate sacrifice when we find ourselves facing moments that require our own sacrifice. Nothing we will ever be asked to give up or walk away from amounts to what Christ gave up for us.

Remembering what the Lord has done for us gives us the capacity to fix our eyes on Him and never allow the things of this world to hold more weight in our life than He does. Everything in our hands has been entrusted to us to steward; it all belongs to God. We need to receive this truth as the foundation under every decision we make. It enables us to live open-handed, with the freedom to release and receive with ease. When I remember how Jesus sacrificed for me, it becomes a little easier to surrender whenever I'm asked. A God who would lay down His life for me, knowing that I would make choices contrary to His plan for me, is worthy of everything I would ever have to give up in my pursuit of Him. Our surrender flows not from a force of will but from receiving God's love for us and responding to His love by living a life poured out, surrendered.

Nothing we will ever be asked to give up or walk away from amounts to what Christ gave up for us.

Surrender isn't a one-time decision. A posture of surrender looks like consistently removing the things that occupy the space in between us and Jesus and moving closer to His plan and His heart each day. This leads us back to Psalm 27:4, the verse I shared at the beginning of this chapter. There should be nothing that I crave beyond living with Jesus. Fellowship with our Lord should be our ultimate desire, and all other things come secondary to that.

God asks us, "Can I be enough for you?" Can your knowledge of who God is be enough for you to surrender and say yes to His leading? If you aren't exactly clear about where this journey will lead you, can God be enough for you to start?

The You That God Knows

Jeremiah 1:5 reads, "Before I formed you in the womb I knew you, before you were born I set you apart; I appointed you as a prophet to the nations" (NIV).

God was asking Jeremiah to do something so far outside himself it felt overwhelming. God was calling him to go and speak to a rebellious people on God's behalf. Jeremiah responded to the invitation with the reasons he wasn't the one. He started to consider the things that disqualified him from what God was calling him to do. He told God these things about himself as if God weren't the one who created him. Does this response sound familiar to you? Often our hesitation about the journey is rooted in our lack of trust in the One who knows us better than we know ourselves. I would love to tell you that we can develop deep trust in God before He asks us to follow Him into the unknown, but that isn't the case. Surrendering and saying yes to Him when we don't know how things will turn out is what builds trust. The One calling you knows you best. Everything God has planted within you will be revealed as you say yes. And as a result, you, too, will discover the version of you that God knows.

Beginning with the Voice of God

So, where do we take the first step? We begin with what God has said to us.

I know that can be an intimidating beginning—and one that leads us to more questions: *How do I even know if I can hear the voice of God? What if the thing I think God is saying is really me and not Him?*

First, let me confirm without a doubt that, yes, God speaks to you and, yes, you can hear His voice.

My sheep hear My voice, and I know them, and they follow Me. (John 10:27, NKJV)

If we follow Jesus, we hear His voice.

The real issue is usually our lack of awareness of God's voice. It takes time and practice to grasp what God sounds like. Maybe we don't recognize the voice or we mistake it for our own thoughts.

The first way to train your ear to hear the voice of God is by reading the Bible. This is where we discover how God speaks, His cadence and tone, and the different methods He uses. He doesn't always speak the same way to everyone. I love that about God! We can never put Him in a box. He never changes, but He is always in every way revealing another side or layer of who He is—even when He speaks.

He never changes, but He is always in every way revealing another side or layer of who He is—even when He speaks.

One of my favorite stories is the first time Samuel heard the voice of God. Samuel was raised in the house of the Lord by the prophet Eli. One night Samuel was awakened because he kept hearing his name called.

> The lamp of God had not yet gone out, and Samuel was lying down in the house of the LORD, where the ark of God was. Then the LORD called Samuel.
>
> Samuel answered, "Here I am." And he ran to Eli and said, "Here I am; you called me."
>
> But Eli said, "I did not call; go back and lie down." So he went and lay down.
>
> Again the LORD called, "Samuel!" And Samuel got up and went to Eli and said, "Here I am; you called me."
>
> "My son," Eli said, "I did not call; go back and lie down."
>
> Now Samuel did not yet know the LORD: The word of the LORD had not yet been revealed to him.
>
> A third time the LORD called, "Samuel!" And Samuel got up and went to Eli and said, "Here I am; you called me."
>
> Then Eli realized that the LORD was calling the boy. So Eli told Samuel, "Go and lie down, and if he calls you, say, 'Speak,

LORD, for your servant is listening.'" So Samuel went and lay down in his place.

The LORD came and stood there, calling as at the other times, "Samuel! Samuel!"

Then Samuel said, "Speak, for your servant is listening." (1 Samuel 3:3–10, NIV)

What I love so much about this story is that it presents a practical response to hearing God's voice. At first, when Samuel heard his name being called, he assumed it was Eli. Many of us haven't recognized that we have been hearing God's voice all along. Have you ever made the comment "Something told me to do . . ." or even spoken about your intuition letting you know something without having proof? Well, those can be signs that God is speaking to us, but we have minimized them and forgotten that we have the Holy Spirit within us.

Samuel running to Eli reminds us to seek wise counsel. Eli was not only someone that Samuel trusted but also the person that, until this period of time, had been God's voice in Samuel's life. When you are discovering how to hear from God, one of the best ways to start is by seeking wise advice from someone you trust. They should be further along in their faith than you are so they can offer good insight. Asking for their wisdom can be as simple as "I feel like God is saying this to me . . ." A good mentor will have follow-up questions to help you qualify what you heard. They should help you reference Scripture and see how the message you heard aligns with God's character. Last, they should point you back to God Himself to confirm what He's spoken to you. Not only did Eli affirm and make Samuel aware of the fact that God was actually speaking to him, but Eli also gave Samuel instructions on what to do when God called his name again. Samuel heard the voice of God again and, with Eli's guidance, responded, "Speak, for your servant is listening."

A Servant of God First

Man, those are another six words that are game changing in the life of a believer. This, my friend, is our first step: We hear from the Lord, and we respond by offering ourselves ready to listen and serve. We lead with hearts that are open to doing whatever God asks.

Samuel ends up having to say some really tough things to his mentor on God's behalf. Samuel was afraid but understood he was a servant of the Lord, even above being a spiritual son to Eli. I've found myself in similar situations where I've had to share hard things with the people I loved out of obedience to God. I've had to master how to respond as a servant of God first and then as a daughter, sister, or friend.

When I was eighteen years old, I was completely over church. I was burned out and just wanted nothing to do with it anymore. My parents were pastoring a church, and I had been helping with everything for years. But now I was exhausted, and church no longer felt like a place that was building me. I felt like I was building it. I was working at Finish Line, a sneaker store, during this time, and to avoid serving at church, I would pick up extra shifts so I didn't have to go. One day my godmother called, waking me up out of my good Sunday morning sleep, and said, "You are coming to church with me." I went, and it was one of the best days of my life. I joined her church that day. Now, I know that might feel like an impulsive decision, but I felt I heard God as my Father say, "I know they need your gifts and talents at your parents' church, but I can't lose your heart." At this point, I knew God cared more about my soul than my ability to serve. So I chose to follow His presence to the new church, knowing that my decision would at first cause my family some pain. I trusted God would work through any conflict with my parents, though, because I was working to be obedient to Him. Now that I'm thinking about it, that was the first time I had ever heard God speak and then made a decision on my own in response. It was my first journey of yes. What I love about this story is that it didn't matter how far I was drifting. God met me right where I was and led me to the exact place I needed to be.

Well, after the service that day, I went home and explained it to my mom. She was supportive right away. She understood that this was about me following God. I then had to let my dad know. I was scared out of my mind. My decision was already made, and I was asking not for permission but for forgiveness. My mommy and I took my dad to his favorite breakfast spot, we enjoyed a meal, and I told him I had news. I told him I had decided to join another church, which happened to be pastored by one of my dad's friends. My dad did the most unexpected thing: He cried. I was shocked. I didn't think he would be jumping for joy, but I didn't think he would cry. I really didn't know what to do. My mom stepped in and said, "I understand how you feel, but she could be joining a cult and leaving the faith and not just our church." Although it made him sad, his pain didn't override God's word to me. This experience taught me that no matter what, you follow God.

I knew that was only the beginning of what would be required of me throughout life. Possibly I would have to make decisions that would please God but disappoint people, even the ones I love. Whenever doubt or fear creeps in, I pause and ask myself, "What did God say?" This question has become my anchor, especially when life doesn't seem to align with the promises God has spoken over me. It's easy to get distracted by the challenges that come along the way, and sometimes even the voices of those closest to me create doubt when they don't completely understand or agree with the path I'm on.

But I hold on to the words He has spoken, allowing them to keep me clear minded. In moments of uncertainty, reminding myself of what God has said gives me the clarity and strength to keep moving forward. The immediate results of my yes might not always look how I expected, and the journey might not follow a straight line, but going back to His word gives me peace, reminding me that He is faithful. This question—"What did God say?"—helps me refocus, hearing His voice above all others and trusting the process.

In moments of uncertainty, reminding myself of what God has said gives me the clarity and strength to keep moving forward.

All other things pale in comparison with God's word in our lives. My favorite verse that keeps me grounded when I would rather walk away and give up is 1 Corinthians 1:9:

God is faithful [He is reliable, trustworthy and ever true to His promise—He can be depended on], and through Him you were called into fellowship with His Son, Jesus Christ our Lord. (AMP)

In light of this verse, the question "Can God be enough for you?" becomes an invitation to embrace a profound truth: Not only is He enough—He is abundantly more than enough. God is our ultimate source, perfectly worthy of our trust and obedience. But He is also our constant guide, the One who holds us up as we stumble and grow, who gently redirects us when we veer off course. His sufficiency is not just His holiness but His intimate love and steadying presence in every season. As we continue to say yes to Him, we discover that He isn't just waiting at the destination; He is present with us in each step, sustaining us and providing everything we could ever need.

Pause + Reflect

What did God say? This is our first step toward yes when following God's lead. If we don't root ourselves in what He said, our journey will be more difficult than He intended. We have to remind ourselves what God has told us when life, people, or our own worries seem to contradict His word. We have to stand and believe the word from God even when we don't see the full picture.

Take a few minutes and ponder these questions:

1. What did God say to you?

2. What scripture does it remind you of? Is there a Bible verse or story that echoes the message you heard?

3. What do you fear most about what God said?

4. What does the Bible say about this fear?

Here is what I know: The more questions you answer, the more questions arise. It's funny because although we can be quite sure of what God has said, we discover that instructions from Him can often feel like studying a puzzle with missing pieces everywhere. But that's actually the fun part. You get to embark on a partnership with God. The way you will experience Him in this journey will alter your life in the most unexpected and beautiful ways!

2

Where Are We Going?

The LORD had said to Abram, "Leave your native country, your relatives, and your father's family, and go to the land that I will show you."
—Genesis 12:1

When I was growing up, my sister would come into my room and ask, "Do you want to go with me?"

Before I answered her, I always asked, "But where are we going?" And typically, that question led to multiple others, like "How long are we going to be there? Who else is coming? How far away is it?"

Sometimes my sister would answer her own question for me and say, "No, you don't want to go."

My consistent need to question her instead of just saying yes revealed a lack of trust. If I trusted her, I wouldn't need to know all the details. I would just go. It makes me laugh because I recognize that I often find myself asking God the same question: "But where are we going?"

I would love to tell you that whenever God presents me with an instruction, I immediately respond the way Mary, the mother of Jesus, did: with a simple "I am the Lord's servant. May everything you have said about me come true" (Luke 1:38). But even Mary, with her willing heart, had questions of her own (verse 34).

We all have questions, and it's good to ask them. Oftentimes our questions reveal our desire to make sure we really are hearing from God. At our core, we want to do the right thing and please Him. Other times our questions come from the pursuit of perfection, the desire to always get it right. And let me tell you, perfection is a myth that keeps us stagnant. There is a misconception that to follow Jesus, we must pursue a life of perfection. But walking with God is more about progression and discovery. I'm not the same person I was when I embarked on this journey ten years ago. That is a sign of progression. Growth is God's desire for us.

If we could hold on to the reality that life with Jesus is a journey and not a destination, I think we would relinquish our lives to Him far more willingly. Our concern with the where would be overshadowed by the who. Not worrying about perfection but keeping our eyes on walking with Jesus prevents us from becoming distracted by the unknown and instead directs our focus toward what we do know, which is that we are never alone. Saying yes without knowing all the details creates an opportunity to grow in our faith and develop our trust. Proverbs 3:5–6 encourages us:

> Trust in the LORD with all your heart;
> do not depend on your own understanding.
> Seek his will in all you do,
> and he will show you which path to take.

The opposite of trusting the Lord with all my heart is leaning on my own understanding. The concerns revealed in our questions sometimes indicate that we are scrambling to gain our own understanding instead of trusting the Lord.

> *The concerns revealed in our questions sometimes indicate that we are scrambling to gain our own understanding instead of trusting the Lord.*

One of the pep talks I often give myself includes the question "Why not trust God?" If we don't settle into a position of trust, our lives will consistently be uprooted by the unknown and we will ultimately be delayed in reaching our destination. If God is all knowing, we can develop an ability to trust Him even when we don't know all the answers.

The second part of the passage above reminds us that if we include Him in every area of our lives, not just the ones we are comfortable with, then He will make clear which path we should take. This doesn't mean we will have all the answers or even know where it will lead, but what we can trust is that as we seek God, He will direct our way. He can't lead us astray. He leads us only to Him, and in Him is where we experience life beyond our fears.

Of course, we don't just wake up one day and reach this

place of saying yes so easily. It starts with leaning into the Holy Spirit, our advocate and daily companion. He is the one who leads us into all truth (John 16:13).

My "Go" Season

When we start taking obedient steps, one of the first hang-ups we encounter is the temptation to take God's plan and minimize it to fit our understanding. We become confused once events don't go the way we thought they would. We might have perfectly understood the assignment God gave us; we just assumed it would happen the way we envisioned. Take my story, for example.

After I had been living in L.A. for three years, pursuing my dream of being a television producer, a sudden yes led me to a surprising new chapter—serving on staff at a church in Southern California. In 2021, I took on the role of director of communications and experiences and joined the weekend teaching team. This shift was unexpected, taking me from the world of television production and running my own company to preaching the gospel in a local church setting. I hadn't anticipated God's plan to move me so quickly from one season to another, but I leaned into His guidance, knowing He was directing my path.

When life begins to settle and we find ourselves in a rhythm, it's easy to make plans that seem logical and comfortable. We start building according to our vision, not always pausing to ensure our plans align with God's will. But sometimes God calls us out of that comfort, inviting us into a journey that we hadn't foreseen but that will ultimately lead us to a deeper understanding of purpose.

God's plans often exceed what we can imagine, though they don't always come packaged the way we expect. Through the shifts and changes, I've begun to trust His guidance more deeply, knowing that each yes He asks of me prepares me for the next stage He has in mind.

Part of having an intimate relationship with Jesus is that, in time, you become familiar with the ways He speaks to you. It doesn't happen the same way each time, but when God is trying to get my attention, He makes it known through specific means. Before I tell you how God recently uprooted me, I think it's best that I share how I got there. Going back to April 2021, I was in a comfortable rhythm but began to sense that I was about to enter a season of transition yet again. As you know, I like to clear up unknowns as quickly as possible, so the instant I realized God was preparing me for something new, I started working to figure out what He was saying.

I knew in my heart that He was sending me to Nashville because I loved it there. It just made the most sense to me. God was transitioning me to a place that brought me great joy! Ha! I couldn't have been more wrong. I went to visit Nashville, and God made it very clear He wasn't calling me there. This journey of yes often means forsaking our desires and saying yes to God's. Those may sound like tough decisions, but in my experience, they end up being the greatest decisions I've ever made. They always produce a life more fulfilling than if I had chosen to do things my way. In this case, choosing to follow God's voice led me to a dream I didn't even know I had.

Long story short, God moved me from L.A. to the unfamiliar town of Murrieta, California, to join the senior leadership team at Centerpoint Church. He planted me there for almost two years. I didn't know anyone. I went from attending and serving a nondenominational church with predominantly millennial African American members to a large conservative Free Methodist church with a membership that was predominantly Caucasian. It may not have made any sense on paper, but it was the exact thing God wanted me to do.

L.A. is known as the place people go to chase their dreams—a city buzzing with possibilities, where aspirations feel within reach. For me, living in L.A. was all about working in the entertainment industry as a content producer. Less than a year after I launched my production company, though, God had other plans and led me three hours away from the city and its endless resources. It was a move I never would have chosen for myself, but it perfectly aligned with the life He had destined for me.

I was finding success in my production career and making strides in my field, but I had allowed L.A. to shape my identity. My accomplishments had subtly become a distraction, pulling me away from the direction God was nudging me toward: ministry. Looking back, I realize that while L.A. offered me opportunities, it also became a hindrance to the greater purpose God was calling me to fulfill. His way was different, and I finally understood that whether our callings unfold inside the four walls of a church or out in the world, we're all ultimately called to ministry.

At that point in my life, God was guiding me toward the path

I'd been resisting for years. I was comfortable serving Him behind the scenes, helping everything run smoothly, but He saw more in me. He knew there were hidden gifts that could emerge only in a different setting, one that put a demand on those parts of myself I hadn't entirely discovered. Moving away from L.A. and into inland California, I no longer had the noise of constant opportunities and exposure around me. In this quieter space, God was able to reshape my vision of who I was, allowing me to step into a calling I'd previously overlooked.

I originally joined the staff at Centerpoint with the understanding that my role would be behind the scenes. But shortly after I started, I became a dominant voice at church gatherings. I went from hosting during service to preaching frequently. If you had told me back in 2018 that my move to L.A. would set me on a path to becoming a preacher, I would have bet a large sum of money there wasn't an ounce of truth to it.

Here is what I've grown to understand: Sometimes God sends you to a place where the environment calls something new out of you, something you wouldn't have discovered where you were before. That is exactly what happened to me. God changed my environment because the former one was supporting who I was instead of who He was calling me to become. I thought God was sending me to the new church for them, but it turned out the assignment was also for me.

God sees the full picture of our lives, so when He says it's time to go, we must trust Him enough to make the move and rely on the truth that He is with us. It's important to approach life with open hands, remaining ready for God to make changes and call us to new directions.

Later, in January 2023, I was planning to move into a new apartment that was closer to the church and then I was scheduled to be ordained as a pastor in February. My parents, other family members, and friends were all planning to attend my consecration. But while this seemed like the right next step in the trajectory of my life, I didn't have peace about it. One of the barometers of life for me is peace. When I lack peace about a certain thing, it's time for me to seek God on a deeper level about the matter at hand. I never want to make a decision apart from Him, and a lack of peace may be a sign that this move is outside His plan.

So once again, I asked God to give me clarity about why I was feeling conflicted. When you feel apprehension concerning your yes, it's best to confirm it with God. The perfect way to do that is with fasting and prayer. That is exactly what I did. How God chooses to respond is solely based on how He desires to speak to you. Instead of an answer, God met me with a question: "Will you trust Me?"

Although it was posed as a question, it was also an answer. God was telling me, "No matter what this looks like, I got you."

After I said, "Yes, I will trust You," I started to receive instructions. One by one, they came. I remember waiting for the next instruction from God, but it wasn't until I completed the previous step—releasing the new apartment I had been holding on to as a safety net—that God showed me what I needed to do next.

Around this time, I had been trying to reach a friend to get her input on what I was sensing, but for some reason God wouldn't release her to talk about it with me. Well, at 3:57 P.M.

I sent an email to cancel the apartment, and at 4:00 P.M. she called me. I shared with her what I had been hearing God tell me, and she confirmed God had said the same thing to her. That was the final confirmation I needed to keep moving forward.

See, God's voice should hold the most weight. I needed to decide to follow God's voice whether others agreed with it or not. I had to become confident in hearing His voice for myself. This journey of obedience, was less about following God into new experiences and more about stepping into complete dependence on Him. That step of obedience to release the apartment was me saying yes to Him. Once I surrendered, everything started to flow.

Ultimately, God was asking me to take a huge leap and essentially walk away from it all: the apartment, the position, the status, the stability, the knowing—all of it. As much as it shocked me and didn't make sense at the time, it was absolutely aligned with His pattern. God had given me some specific assignments for that year, and staying in my current position was competing with the things He had asked me to focus on. To put it plainly, God was asking for a total surrender. No plan B. So I did it. After about two weeks of instructions and confirmations, I gave my three-week notice, moved out of my apartment, packed my things into storage, and got on a plane heading back home to Chicago. I never thought that God would send me back to Chicago. Thankfully, I landed there for only a few weeks, and then for a full year, I lived as a nomad. Staying in the homes of traveling friends or their parents' rental properties, I traveled between L.A., Chicago, and Atlanta. God always ensured I had a place to comfortably live and rest. My life was turned upside down. I went from stability to complete dependence on God. Here's the kicker: I didn't know the plan. I had only His question: "Will you trust Me?"

The journey of yes consists of these relationship-defining moments when we get the opportunity to choose God over everything else we love and adore. Our decision to obey communicates that the most important thing is pleasing God. Recording artist Steffany Gretzinger often says that God doesn't call us to a certain thing but He calls us to Himself.* I would like to add that God calls us to Himself first, then He calls us to our true selves, which are discovered in Him, and finally He calls us to be an answer for others. When God calls us to follow Him into a new opportunity or assignment, He is really calling us into a deeper communion with Him, which will then be displayed in the place He sends us.

A surprising turn of events—like changing my plans of becoming a pastor and moving—isn't evidence that God changed His mind. It's Him changing the method. We must began to embrace being okay with that. A verse that often helps me embrace seasons of uprooting is Jeremiah 29:11: "'I know the plans I have for you,' declares the LORD, 'plans to prosper you and not to harm you, plans to give you hope and a future'" (NIV). If God has a plan and it's to give us a good future, why

---

* Steffany Gretzinger, quoted in James Lasher, "How to Be Good Stewards of Worship with Steffany Gretzinger," Charisma News, May 19, 2023, charisma news.com/culture/how-to-be-good-stewards-of-worship-with-steffany -gretzinger.

wouldn't we make the decision to follow Him? He knows best. I may not know exactly where I'm going, but I do know that God's call will lead me down a good path.

A mentor once told me, "God is going to teach you what it means to live by faith." Let me tell you, she did not lie. Every journey of yes has taken me into deeper dependence on Him.

This decision for me to give my three weeks' notice and change my plans completely wasn't an easy one. Sometimes it's easy to say yes to God when you are making a choice between right and wrong, darkness and light. But what happens when God is asking you to choose between two things that seem to be good? Even if the good thing serves Him—like ministering in a church—if it isn't what He is asking you to say yes to, it's no longer the right thing for you.

The truth that helped me in this season was that when God calls us to move, His grace is always going before us. I recognized that the grace for my current assignment was lifting and God was transitioning me to something new. As comfortable as I was, I was equally unsettled. God will never let you rest in a place where you no longer belong. I couldn't afford to stay where there was no grace. But it can be challenging to distinguish between a shift in grace and our own frustrations. So I embarked on a four-day fast and asked the Lord to search my heart and reveal any hidden issues that might obstruct my ability to hear Him clearly. Additionally, I surrendered my desired outcomes during this fast. This is crucial because we often approach God asking Him to bless our own plans rather than seeking His desires for us. By laying my thoughts and desires before Him, I was able to listen, observe, and discern whether God's grace rested on the current situation or He was calling me to move on.

The Ripple Effect

When we refuse to give God a yes, it doesn't just affect us. Your answer will create a ripple effect that will have an impact on everyone connected to you. Let me explain. If I had made the choice to go against God and stay at Centerpoint, I would have become a blockage for what needed to flow in the space I refused to leave. When God transitions you into a new season, you aren't the only one. Pride tempts us to believe God is moving only us. But He also has plans for the people and the spaces you're leaving.

When God transitions you into a new season, you aren't the only one. He also has plans for the people and the spaces you're leaving.

We can't allow our ego to deceive us into thinking that our decision to disobey is about the people or the responsibilities in our current situation. When God transitions us, we oftentimes ask, "What about all the things and people I'm leaving behind? What will they think about my decision? How will they feel?" It's almost as if we are worrying more about God's people than He does.

I struggled with my decision for a while because I felt like I would cause pain to people who wouldn't understand why another one of their pastors was leaving. I didn't want to abandon them. But when I laid these questions before God, I recognized I had begun to serve my position over the One who put me there in the first place. I was where I was only because God sent me, which meant He always had a plan and that wouldn't change because I was leaving. I had to ask myself a tough question: *Is my fear of the unknown masked as concern?* Yes, I was concerned. I absolutely cared about the fallout of my decision to leave that church, but sometimes we can allow those emotions to hide our fear of the unknown. All these things led me right back to God's original question: "Will you trust Me?" God was asking if I would trust Him to handle it all: my life, as well as the lives affected by my decision to follow Him.

I've discovered that whether I've heard from God is often confirmed by the fruit of my decision. We may not see it right away, but we will be able to see Him working all things together. We often want to see the fruit before we start the journey, and that will never be possible. Even in the natural world, there is time and process before we see the fruit that comes from a planted seed. One step of obedience leads to the next, and over time we experience the fruit of our choice to follow God even when we were unsure.

The verse that my spiritual father always reminds me of during times of transition is Psalm 37:23: "The steps of a good man are ordered by the LORD, and He delights in his way" (NKJV).

We might read the word *ordered* and think somehow our steps will be planned for us and we'll know them all, but in its original language, that word means "erected, established."* As we take one step, another step will arise, and another, and so forth. The fact that another instruction is revealed after you obey the first one is a good sign that you're being faithful to a God that has promised to fulfill His word concerning you (Hebrews 10:23).

Holy Disruption

When I'm embarking on a journey, before I take the first step, I often ask God to give me confirmation. Seasons of transition can be sensitive, so we have to make sure we are alert and aware that at any point God can be speaking. During this time, He used two men: one to speak to my uncertainty and the other to speak to my need to trust God even when a decision feels impulsive. The week before my last Sunday at Centerpoint Church, I went to a worship night at a friend's church. I thought I was just going to sit in the back, receive, and leave. Little did I know God had a plan to seal this journey I was about to embark on.

It was an awesome service; things were normal until they weren't. When it came to an end, the pastor called my name and mentioned that the Lord had spoken to him about me

* "Strong's H3559—Kûn," Blue Letter Bible, accessed November 12, 2024, blueletterbible.org/lexicon/h3559/kjv/wlc/0-1.

weeks ago! He didn't know when he was supposed to share until I mentioned I was coming to this service, so God released him to do it that night. The fact that God had spoken to him weeks ago shocked me in the best way. He shared that God was moving me, and he emphasized, "I heard God's voice and that His grace and power need no explanation."

Before this encounter, I had felt unsure about the decisions I was making and a bit impulsive. They felt so out of the box and even irresponsible. God knew exactly what I needed to hear. I felt secure in moving forward, and the Lord kept reassuring me that this was the direction He wanted me to go. One day a pastor at Centerpoint came up to me and reminded me of Romans 8:14: "For all who are *allowing themselves* to be led by the Spirit of God are sons of God" (AMP, emphasis added). That was a turning point, and this verse has since become a security blanket for me.

I was grateful for God's intentionality. He revealed a word to someone for me weeks before He called me to move, then used a trusted voice in real time to confirm what He said. My obedience led me right into a defining moment and gave me the sense of peace I needed to take the first step. I felt safe jumping off a cliff into God's call to trust Him. If I'd had to make all these seemingly irrational decisions alone without confirmation from God, it would have been so hard.

These reassurances eased so much of the frustration and resentment I'd been feeling because I couldn't explain the rationale of God's call on my life to others. One of the best pieces of advice that my spiritual father shared with me is that God's assignments aren't conference calls. Our relationship with

Jesus isn't a democracy. We can't wait for our friends and family to agree with us before we make the decision to follow Him. Your journey, while it will influence others, requires only your participation, not anyone else's understanding. Some won't understand until they experience the fruit of your decision to follow God.

> *We can't wait for our friends and family to agree with us before we make the decision to follow Him.*

We often feel alone in our journeys of obedience, but I find comfort in the Bible, God's Word. There is always a story of someone on a journey like the one God is calling me into. And we know that God doesn't change. He is the same yesterday, today, and forevermore (Hebrews 13:8). Which means that how He showed up for them, He can show up for you and me. Take Abraham, for example.

Before Abraham received a name change and promises that are still being fulfilled through our lives today, he was just Abram. Then one day God called him into the journey of yes that would ultimately change his life and ours:

> The LORD had said to Abram, "Go from your country, your people and your father's household to the land I will show you.

"I will make you into a great nation,
and I will bless you;
I will make your name great,
and you will be a blessing.
I will bless those who bless you,
and whoever curses you I will curse;
and all peoples on earth
will be blessed through you."
So Abram went, as the LORD had told him.
(Genesis 12:1–4, NIV)

God asked Abram to uproot himself from his people and his father's household and walk away from the stability and comfort of everything he knew. The crazy part is that God didn't tell him where to go. He just said, "Let's go, and I will show you when we get there." This is the epitome of trusting God and not leaning on your own understanding. This was such an irrational decision to make, yet as we follow God's leading, we can't allow our limited logic to direct us away from His ultimate plan. Our ways aren't God's ways, and our thoughts aren't His either (Isaiah 55:8). We must receive His instruction and not dilute it with our human perspective, or we will never experience all He has for us.

When God told him to go, Abraham was seventy-five years old. His life was established; he was known in the area. He and his family had responsibilities, yet God said it was time to walk away from it all.

Following God's lead often means a disruption to what

seems sensible to us. It's not always a movement from one place to the next, as it was with Abraham and me. Sometimes God calls us to stay and put down roots. It all boils down to obedience and asking yourself, *What does God require of me now?*

What I love about Abraham's story is that although God didn't say where they were going, He shared what He would do. It's almost like He started this conversation saying, "I know I'm asking you to walk away from everything, but let Me reveal everything I have for you." I can certainly say even in my life I've known the simple truth that nothing I leave behind will ever be better than what God walks me into. Abram trusted God more than he feared what he didn't know. After God shared the promises with Abram, he packed his family up and did as the Lord asked him.

Abram, who later became known as Abraham, is celebrated as the father of faith. His willingness to follow God made him one of the most influential figures in the Bible, and through him, God planted the seeds that would form the nation of Israel and result in the coming of Jesus Himself.

Abraham's story illustrates the profound rewards of saying yes to God. One significant reward was the personal relationship he developed with God. Abraham interceded for the city of Sodom, pleading with God to spare it if a certain number of righteous people could be found in it (Genesis 18:16–33). Although only a few people were saved and the city was destroyed, Abraham's ability to engage in such a heartfelt dialogue with God reveals the depth of their relationship. Becoming a friend of God is the greatest reward of saying yes, highlighting the intimate connection and influence one can have through obedience.

Throughout the following chapters in Genesis, we see God continue to define the relationship between Himself and Abraham. After you meet someone, there's a point where all the phone conversations, dates, and text messages need a definition. Where is this going? You need an agreement of intentionality. You want to know if this is headed toward a committed relationship, a friendship, or nothing at all. Similarly, God wants us to be sure our trust in Him isn't tied to our expectations being met. If a situation doesn't turn out how we thought it would, will we still worship and serve God, or is His lordship real to us only if we get what we want from Him?

God promised Abraham wonderful things, but Abraham understood that saying yes to God meant staying faithful to Him, rather than focusing on the blessings. God gave Abraham a son and promised he would become the father of many nations (17:4). However, God later asked Abraham to take his son Isaac up a mountain and sacrifice him (22:1–19)—a request that defies human logic and would be considered a crime in modern society. Despite the confusing nature of this command, Scripture tells us that Abraham rose early the next morning and set out to follow God's instruction. This immediate obedience highlights the importance of relationship: Although Abraham didn't know what the outcome would be, he trusted in God's faithfulness and goodness. Abraham was so confident in God's character that he left his servants at the base of the mountain, telling them, "We will worship and then *we* will come back to you" (verse 5, NIV, emphasis added). It's through a deep relationship with God that we find the faith to say yes, even when the task seems impossible.

We choose to follow God not because of what we will get out of it but because of who He is and will always be. That is why whenever God asked me to follow Him into a new thing, my desire to know where I was going began to lose validity. I started to see that the only thing that matters is *who* is leading the way. All that matters is that God is with me.

We choose to follow God not because of what we will get out of it but because of who He is and will always be.

Pause + Reflect

Hebrews 11:8 reads, "By faith Abraham, when called to go to a place he would later receive as his inheritance, obeyed and went, even though he did not know where he was going" (NIV).

This verse lays out our blueprint. Our faith gives us the ability to obey God even when we don't know all the details. Remember, we don't wait for all the steps to appear; as we take each step, the next one is revealed.

You may not have all the details or know specifically where God will lead you. But God is with you. He isn't trying to disrupt your life just to be a puppet master. Any step away from something is a step toward something greater than what you are leaving behind. You may not know where you are going, but who you are going with is all that matters.

Any step away from something is a step toward something greater than what you are leaving behind.

Reflect and ask yourself the following questions:

1. What is God asking you to do?

2. Where haven't you gone because you were too concerned with the details of the destination and what others thought about the change?

3. What if you never know all the details?

4. In what ways have you obeyed the voice of fear over the voice of God? And in what ways have you obeyed the voice of God over the voice of fear?

3

The Cost

Don't begin until you count the cost. For who would begin
construction of a building without first calculating the cost
to see if there is enough money to finish it?
—Luke 14:28

For as long as I can remember, I've been a person who
weighs the options and what each will cost me before I
make a commitment. Growing up, I would always determine
what my punishment would be if I chose to do something
I knew was wrong and if it was worth the cost or not. Most of
the time, I felt like I didn't want to miss out on the experience,
so I chose to suffer the consequences. Usually I would tell on
myself; I earned the punishment. It makes me laugh now because what kind of child just decides, *Let's do it. This is worth
the punishment I will receive?* But I've noticed that I still default to the same approach when it comes to saying yes to
God. *What will it cost me to follow God's lead? Is it worth everything I will lose?*

No matter where we are on the journey, the answers will
mostly be the same.

What will it cost? Our life.

Is it worth it? Absolutely.

I'm very aware that I don't know the details of your life and what you might stand to lose on this journey of yes. But I will say nothing in your life is a matchup for God. Sometimes it can be hard to choose Him over the tangible things we experience each day, but I promise you, there will never be another thing or person as consistent in your life as God.

I don't want to lie to you or play into the misconception that because we have made the choice to follow Jesus, life gets easier. It will not. Life will just make us more and more dependent on Jesus. Experiencing loss—whether of things, people, positions, or dreams—can be some of the toughest times in our lives. However, if we are to embrace the fullness of life that God has in store for us, we must be willing to let go of anything that takes His place in our hearts. Our highest ambition in life should be to please God. If that is the case, then the things we have to walk away from shouldn't faze us as much, because our trust in God and His character is stronger. The gift of obedience becomes what I gain through my loss. That can look different for all of us. Sometimes it's the lessons along the way that become our gain. Other times it can be the realization that what we were clinging to was actually hurting us more than it was growing us. The thing we must trust is that while we are aware only of who we are currently, God sees us in our totality. God knows who we are to become. The journeys that He has predestined for us are aligned with that complete version of ourselves.

While we are aware only of who we are currently, God sees us in our totality.

A Test of Faith

Knowing that not everyone will agree with my decision to say yes comes with the acceptance that not everyone will take the journey either. The path God calls us to walk is deeply personal, and while it may be hard to let go of the need for others' approval or company, saying yes often means trusting Him to guide us, even when the journey requires walking alone for a season. Your yes will transform every aspect of your life, including your relationships. During a period that tested my relationships, I found encouragement in the book of James. I came to see that a life with Jesus often involves suffering, but purpose is always found in that suffering. Our faith deepens as we are tested and embrace seeking God beyond the journeys that feel rewarding.

> Dear brothers and sisters, when troubles of any kind come your way, consider it an opportunity for great joy. For you know that when your faith is tested, your endurance has a chance to grow. So let it grow, for when your endurance is fully developed, you will be perfect and complete, needing nothing. (1:2–4)

As I sat with this scripture, I wanted to know how I would be able to find joy in what was crushing me. One random week turned out to be a game-changing milestone in my life. I later realized this week happened to be one year after I made the decision to walk away from my job at Centerpoint. At the start of the week, I was on a Zoom call with a missionary organization, encouraging their leaders. While on the call, they gave testimonies about how God was moving on college campuses as a result of their tour. A young woman shared a story of how they met a student who felt a strong conviction about not joining a sorority. Although her parents practically cut her off for the decision, she knew deep down she wasn't supposed to join. That was definitely her journey of yes, one that cost her approval from her parents. As I listened, I realized the organization wasn't in agreement with Greek sororities and fraternities, and at the time, I was a member of a sorority, specifically a Black Greek-letter organization. I didn't really think too deeply of the conversation. It wasn't my first time hearing people of faith speak out against organizations similar to ones I was a member of. I didn't feel I had done anything to go against my faith in Jesus Christ, but the Holy Spirit was about to reveal some heavy truths to me before the end of the week.

I continued through the week as I normally would. Friday came, and I was preparing to have a podcast interview with a young woman by the name of Pavielle on her show, *The Purpose Collective*. As you can infer from the podcast title, the topic of discussion was purpose. God had a plan, and He was determined to lead me into a freedom I didn't know I needed.

Pavielle asked me how I knew I was called, and for the first time ever in telling that story, I almost mentioned how I pledged a sorority in college and later, while still in undergrad, felt like God wanted me to denounce the sorority. I didn't say it out loud, but I was just as shocked as if I had. I asked myself, *Where did that come from? It's not a part of the story I normally share.* We got further into the conversation, and Pavielle mentioned that she had recently renounced the sorority she was a part of after receiving the Holy Spirit. She mentioned it a couple of times within the interview, and I started an internal discussion with God, asking Him what He was trying to tell me. Remember, this was the second time in the same week that the topic of sororities and fraternities had come up. We wrapped up the podcast, and I asked Pavielle what sorority she was a part of. Coincidentally, it was the same organization I was a member of. She shared in depth her journey and how the Holy Spirit revealed things to her about the sorority that led her to renounce her pledge. She had even recorded a full podcast episode about it. I asked her to send the link to me. She was also proactive in sending me a template letter of renunciation that she hoped I would eventually use.

A week or so went by, and the truth is, I never intended to listen to the podcast. I was a bit annoyed that Pavielle kept bringing it up. In hindsight I recognize that our responses to things can often clue us into areas of bondage we aren't even aware of. I was driving home when the Holy Spirit told me to play the podcast, and less than twenty minutes into it, I was weeping. I realized that, thirteen years ago, I had unknowingly entered a demonic covenant. The weird thing is, I couldn't remember much of that pledge ceremony and what is known as crossing the sands. But the instant I listened to the podcast, those memories resurfaced, and my heart was so grieved. I had said things that felt harmless at the time, but in reality, God wasn't pleased.

In short, each of the Divine Nine organizations has a god or goddess associated with it as the emblem of that organization. In the initiation process, we are led to take an oath in front of a ceremonial table with a burning candle, ultimately coming into covenant with a false deity.

The Bible is extremely clear on what the Lord thinks about idols:

You must not have any other god but me. (Exodus 20:3)

And what union can there be between God's temple and idols? For we are the temple of the living God. As God said:

"I will live in them
and walk among them.
I will be their God,
and they will be my people." (2 Corinthians 6:16)

These verses summed up the reason I had no other option but to tell the Lord yes. I would sever ties with a covenant I had made unknowingly. Even just thinking about it right now makes me so emotional because I'm overwhelmed to think I made a vow to anything outside my Lord and Savior. It's the absolute mercy of God that would pursue us in our known and unknown sin and bring us back into righteous standing with Him.

It's the absolute mercy of God that would pursue us in our known and unknown sin and bring us back into righteous standing with Him.

After listening to the podcast and deciding to renounce the organization, I repented the entire drive home and cried out to the Lord to forgive me. I honestly had no idea what I had really done by joining the organization. I was twenty years old and nowhere near as mature in my faith.

I sent the letter to the national headquarters, officially renouncing my pledge and asking for my name to be removed from their roll. There is only one book I want my name recorded in, and that is the Lamb's book of life.

Following God's lead will reveal truths that cost us things we once held dear. We have to be okay with letting things go, trusting that His ways are far better for us in the end.

No Other Gods

The scary part about all of this is we can have no idea we are serving idols, because idolatry is so pervasive in our culture. We have to ask the Holy Spirit to give us wisdom and to increase our discernment so that we become aware when we dethrone God and enthrone something else within our hearts.

It's easy to assume an idol is only something we physically worship or something that disrupts our religious practices, like attending church or reading the Bible. However, an idol can be anything we hold dear, apart from God. Our family, our job, and our hobbies can all become idols if they take a place in our hearts alongside or even above God.

That's why it's important to invite the Holy Spirit into this journey with you. The Holy Spirit guides us into all truth John 16:13). Asking God to help you identify the idols in your life can reveal the things in your heart that you may be unknowingly serving.

Many times in Scripture, God would test the hearts of those He loved to reveal the real objects of their affection (Psalm 7:9; Jeremiah 17:10). What do you love the most? Is it your influence, your position at work, your money, your children, or your spouse? What in your life would cause you to waver in your commitment to God? These things I listed, as you know, aren't bad things, but when we begin to serve them instead of or above God, we have crossed a line.

One of the Scripture passages that always realigns my heart posture is the story of the rich young ruler:

> A man came running up to him, knelt down, and asked, "Good Teacher, what must I do to inherit eternal life?"
>
> "Why do you call me good?" Jesus asked. "Only God is truly good. But to answer your question, you know the commandments: 'You must not murder. You must not commit adultery. You must not steal. You must not testify falsely. You must not cheat anyone. Honor your father and mother.'"

"Teacher," the man replied, "I've obeyed all these commandments since I was young."

Looking at the man, Jesus felt genuine love for him. "There is still one thing you haven't done," he told him. "Go and sell all your possessions and give the money to the poor, and you will have treasure in heaven. Then come, follow me."

At this the man's face fell, and he went away sad, for he had many possessions. (Mark 10:17–22)

What stands out the most in this story is that the rich young ruler walked away sad. Much like him, we enter a relationship with God with a willingness to know what it really costs to follow Him wholeheartedly. But when God begins to lay out the things we need to give up, we are saddened. Some of us have walked away. Even when we think we are doing all the right things, our hearts can be far from God and owned by something else.

Remember, earlier we talked about the importance of trust. This is one of the times when we need it the most, because God asking us to give something up is an act of love, not war. He isn't trying to ruin us. He is trying to eliminate the distance created when we allow things to stand between our hearts and His.

God asking us to give something up is an act of love, not war.

The Bible tells us that He is a jealous God (Exodus 34:14). Rightfully so. He paid a high price for us. For us to lend our hearts to things that can do absolutely nothing for us is a slap in the face of a holy God who made the ultimate sacrifice. And most times we are unaware that our hearts are tied to other things until He starts to ask for them. Jesus wasn't trying to take away the wealth and success of the rich young ruler. He was after his heart. Likewise, Jesus isn't interested in us doing things for Him just to check a box. He wants our hearts. We have to get to a place where we will forsake anything that will hinder our intimacy with Jesus.

That choice is easier in some areas of my life than in others. I can often handle God transitioning me from one place to another, because that is a pattern I've come to accept. It's the way God has fashioned me to live out my calling. When my decision to lay down a thing to follow Jesus affects the lives of others, though, I struggle. Ultimately I choose Jesus, but sometimes it's in a delayed-obedience kind of way, which is still disobedience. When I have clarity about what God is asking me to do but still allow the fear of man to stagnate me, I've chosen to be disobedient. Now, I don't want to eliminate the space we often need to count the cost. Obeying God is also a process. There is a difference between stalling out of fear and ensuring you are following the voice of God. Usually my delayed obedience is connected to not wanting to disappoint people. I'm not going to make excuses, but it's a weighty thing when our choices unravel the lives of those who didn't set out to join our journey.

For this reason and so many others, it's so important to have the right people in your life. You need to have people who will support the journey even if they don't entirely understand it. I think about the last couple of years and how my parents and inner circle were pillars that held me through some of the riskiest faith moves. They may not have always understood the decisions I made, but they trusted that I was hearing from God and respected my journey of obedience. In my circle of friends, we each have unique callings and assignments, and our purposes unfold differently. However, we are all committed to surrendering to God in the ways He desires for us. It's easier to follow God when your community is also following Him. Having a group that prioritizes God's word over our own thoughts, wills, or emotions often helps support and affirm our obedience to God.

You, too, need people in your corner. Seek a community that collectively embraces doing whatever it takes to please God.

Seek a community that collectively embraces doing whatever it takes to please God.

After I decided to part ways with the Divine Nine organization, I recognized that God was calling me to speak up about it. Initially I was so annoyed by this because I knew what it was going to cost. It was going to come across to some as though I was picking a fight, and technically I was. I was righteously angered that I had been deceived and thought about how many others had become engaged in something that went against God but had no clue. But I wanted no part in shaking things up. A conversation was already happening, and I would only be adding my perspective to the mix. People were renouncing and denouncing every day. My friends and ministry peers were seeing the light. I would have been okay with supporting them with my silent agreement. Then God said, "Not so." He was asking me not only to take a stand but also to speak up, and He wasn't having it any other way.

The day I listened to the podcast and sent in my letter, I shared on Instagram Stories in tears how God had revealed to me what I had done by becoming a member of this organization and how heartbroken I was. The next day, I did a podcast interview on a large platform, and I knew there was no turning back. In full disclosure, I was aware of how hot the topic was, but I had no idea that God was going to breathe on the content to ensure people would be set free. For every bit of negative feedback, there was a comment or a message where someone shared either how my testimony led them to make a similar decision or that they were choosing not to pledge because it was confirmation that God didn't want them involved. For all these people, I'm grateful. Still, going public with my story rubbed others the wrong way. People who had supported me in other steps of obedience found fault because my yes exposed things they wanted to keep quiet about. I'm now okay with that, but it took some time and tears to get there.

Through this experience, I discovered the part of me that still cared what others thought about what I did. Deep in my heart, I desired the people I loved and respected to agree with me about what God was asking me to do. But God taught me that His word is the only agreement I need.

> Fear of man will prove to be a snare,
> but whoever trusts in the LORD is kept safe.
> (Proverbs 29:25, NIV)

These simple words hold so much weight in my heart. I can't allow my fear of what others will think or say to withhold my yes from Jesus.

It's never okay to fear people more than we honor God. The enemy is always looking to lead us away from God. He will exploit our preoccupation with the approval of others every chance he gets, sending people you love and respect to plant seeds of doubt in your subconscious that will sprout over time and cause you to shrink back from what God is calling you to. That's exactly what was happening to me. I was doubting the things God said and called me to do, because the people I loved didn't understand.

Sometimes others express resistance out of love, or sometimes their pushback has nothing to do with you personally. People will weigh the cost of your journey and decide that it would be too much for them. Or out of their love for you and desire to protect you, they will project their fear onto you and try to convince you to keep quiet. That's kind of funny because the most unsafe place you can reside is outside the will of God.

Here's a truth: Those who play it safe don't make an impact on the world.

I had to stand in the boldness rooted in the truth that if Jesus is leading me this way, even if I have to go alone, all of heaven is backing me. Not because of who I am, but because this journey aligns with His will and establishing His kingdom on earth. A life of surrender will produce a growing comfort with not wasting time trying to prove and explain ourselves but allowing the fruit of our yes to speak.

Those you love may never agree or even understand, but saying yes to Jesus means you forsake everything and everyone and follow Him. Have courage, because you don't make this decision in fear. You say yes in full confidence that Jesus has you covered. He will never ask you to pay a cost without seeing His goodness on the other side.

> *Those you love may never agree or even understand, but saying yes to Jesus means you forsake everything and everyone and follow Him.*

All who have left houses, brothers, sisters, father, mother, children, or farms because of my name will receive one hundred times more and will inherit eternal life. (Matthew 19:29, CEB)

Pause + Reflect

This is where you count the cost. Considering all the costs before choosing to say yes to Jesus is an act of faith but will help you guard against things that will compete with Him for your attention. On your journey of yes, you will surrender all things to the lordship of Jesus Christ. You will put Jesus over everything. To follow Jesus is to make the decision that nothing holds more weight than Him.

Make space to practice honesty with God. One of my favorite scriptures to pray is the passage below:

> Search me [thoroughly], O God, and know my heart;
> Test me and know my anxious thoughts;
> And see if there is any wicked or hurtful way in me,
> And lead me in the everlasting way. (Psalm 139:23–24, AMP)

Take some time to think through the questions below, and consider what things, relationships, positions, or environments are possibly holding the place only Jesus should ever occupy in your life:

1. What things in your life would be difficult to live without?

2. What has God asked you to release that you are struggling to let go of?

3. What will it cost you if you say yes and give up that thing?

4. What are you saying no to while you cling to something other than what God has called you to? (For example, how many people wouldn't have experienced freedom through hearing my testimony if I had remained silent?) Whatever the Lord is requiring you to surrender in this season, I promise it will cost more to *not* yield it than it ever would to say yes.

4

When Yes Leads to the Unexpected

Peter called to him, "Lord, if it's really you, tell me to come
to you, walking on the water."
—Matthew 14:28

Journeys are breeding grounds for the unexpected.

When we take a trip, we know to prepare for—and even
expect—any number of surprises. There is always the possibility of delays, lost luggage, or canceled plans. I wonder why
it's difficult for us to apply that same awareness to our spiritual journeys.

Somewhere in our minds, we assume that following Jesus
includes the assurance that the road ahead will be smooth,
without trials or plot twists. But that isn't what life with Christ
is about. In fact, the moment we say yes to Jesus, life gets real.
To be a follower of Jesus who is obedient and acknowledges
Him as Lord is to become a threat to the kingdom of darkness.
That means we will inevitably face trials. Jesus tells us,

> I have told you all this so that you may have peace in me. Here
> on earth you will have many trials and sorrows. But take heart,
> because I have overcome the world. (John 16:33)

*The moment we say yes to Jesus,
life gets real.*

There will be trials—*and* peace in the midst of the hard things we walk through. To say yes to God means we will experience surprises, and some of those surprises will be hard. Highs, lows, ups, downs, mountains, valleys—all the above are included in the journey. But the gift we have is knowing without a doubt that Jesus is with us every step of the way. His presence doesn't ensure life will be without pain. It ensures that as we experience the pain, we have a comforter with us. No matter what the pain intended to do, the Holy Spirit will guide and comfort us throughout the journey (John 14:16–17, AMP).

I don't mean to come across as if I've mastered expecting the unexpected. I've decided to accept that the unexpected will occur. But the trick about the unexpected is that you can never prepare for it. It will always take you by surprise.

I grew up as a pastor's kid, so I grew up in church. I later discovered that didn't mean I was growing in relationship with Jesus. For as long as I can remember, church was a consistent part of my life. It was a part of my weekly schedule right along with school and extracurricular activities. My life revolved around church: I served in church, I led small groups, I was a ministry leader, I created ministries, and I served my pastors. And yet, with all that activity, I didn't have a tangible relationship with Jesus. I knew of God, but I didn't know God intimately.

Whenever I reflect on this time in my life, I always think of it as my journey to God's heart, because it gave me the capacity to understand the way He loves us. Romans 8 tells us nothing can separate us from the love of God (verses 38–39). There is nothing we can do to make Him love us more or less. There is nothing we can do to earn His love. It's a gift, and He personified that gift by sending us Jesus. And because Jesus bore all our shortcomings and sins—anything that might separate us from God—when God looks at us, He sees us through the work that Jesus completed on the cross. Not only does God love us unconditionally, but we are also required to love one another the way that He loves us. I understood that no matter what I do, God doesn't change His mind about me. He doesn't change the way He loves me. He doesn't change the way He interacts with me. His heart toward me remains the same. And the reason I say that is, in contrast, the people I loved betrayed me in a way that completely devastated me and shook the foundations my life was built on. Yet God gave me the ability to love them in spite of that. I had compassion and empathy where I should have been angry and bitter. Where I should have been seeking revenge, I found myself reflecting God's heart toward them.

When Everything Changed

In January 2018, I found myself wanting to grow deeper in intimacy with Jesus. I was on staff full time at a church. I was also leading a young adult ministry that had experienced some substantial growth, and it was shifting the culture of the church. God was stretching me, and for the first time, I was open to following Him wherever He wanted to lead. I was really, really locked in with the Lord, and I wanted more of Him. I felt like He was pulling me closer, so I started the year off shutting everything down and committing to the Daniel Fast. I was taking a prayer class at that time and decided to take God's purpose and plan for my life seriously. I felt like one of my friends, Alex (not his real name), was being highlighted to me in a deeper capacity than friendship. To be honest, it completely caught me off guard. Here I was pursuing the Lord, and He starts bringing my friend to mind. I genuinely loved Alex, but like a brother, so when I started to consider him romantically, I thought, *Okay, God. You're going to have to make this plain. You're going to have to shift how we see each other.* During the time of fasting, God wasn't specifically saying, "This is going to be your husband." But I noticed that something was shifting and we possibly had deeper feelings for each other. When I sought God concerning Alex and me, all I received was a simple instruction: *Pray for him.*

Sometimes God gives us only bits and pieces without any context because if we had insight, our flesh would hinder our obedience. In these instances, we oftentimes follow our desires and shift God's instructions to align with what we want instead of what He said. We like to do things our way.

I did pray for Alex, but I also started to step outside God's timing. Alex and I hung out often because we shared a friend group and worked at the same church. We both recognized that the dynamics of our friendship had begun to change, and by the end of the month, we were basically in a relationship. When you are friends with someone for ten years, you get to skip all the "what's your favorite color" conversations. We already had the foundation of a close friendship, and it was easy to build from there. Had our relationship continued, we more than likely would have been married by the following year. It was moving fast. If I'm completely honest, that was probably the first time I had been in love deeply. I jumped in headfirst because he was one of my best friends and I didn't have my guard up. In my mind, there was no way my best friend could hurt me.

In hindsight, I recognize how our focus was diverted from building intimacy with God to getting to know each other. Because God was the center of our lives individually, we felt like He automatically became the center of our relationship. That wasn't true. I can't speak for Alex, but I lost sight of God within the relationship. I don't think I ever consulted with Him concerning the progression of our relationship. I can't recall myself asking, "God, are You in this?" I didn't include Him in *everything*.

One day, Alex and I were working at church when I came across a text message on his phone. You know when you set your phone on the table and don't lock it? Well, that's how I saw the text message, which was absolutely inappropriate for someone who was in a relationship.

I can remember how I wanted to just forget it and act like what I saw wasn't what I saw, but the Holy Spirit wouldn't allow that. It kept playing in my head on a loop. Long story short, after seeing that text message, I came across a series of other conversations that led me to discover that Alex was in an intimate relationship with my male pastor.

I was close with my pastors; I had a key to their house. The guest room was basically called Brenda's room because I stayed there so often. When they would go out of town, I took care of their two boys. I served as a personal assistant to the wife, who ran the women's ministry and led a small group. She would travel to speak a lot, so I served her in that capacity. Basically, they were like my second parents. I called them Moms and Pops. Not only were we close personally but they were also my spiritual parents. They were my first set of leaders who identified my pastoral leadership gift and gave me opportunities to cultivate it. They allowed me to lead, build, and innovate. To this day, I credit my leadership abilities and skill sets, even the way I understand and communicate the Word, to their leadership.

We need to be able to separate a person's character from choices they made as a result of their brokenness.

I think we need to be able to separate a person's character from choices they made as a result of their brokenness. Wisdom helps us say, "Although this person did this thing to me, it doesn't remove the good they did before." That lesson took some time for me to understand. I had so many opportunities from being under his leadership for so many years. The breach in our trust doesn't take away from how God used this pastor in my life. If we eliminate the good because of the bad, we will miss how God moves and repurposes situations in our lives. Now, were there things this pastor should have done better? Absolutely. Was I heartbroken? One hundred percent. But it doesn't take away from the person that he was to me in the season God ordained us to be connected.

All have sinned and fall short of the glory of God.
(Romans 3:23, NIV)

The Yes That Heals

To extend mercy, we have to understand our need for that same mercy. We all have sinned and come short of the glory of God (Romans 3:23). We will always be in need of grace. That is the reality of our lives. And I think that a part of my empathy came from knowing I, too, am a broken person and have caused others pain. The forgiveness and mercy that I so need, I also had the capacity to give. I felt that way immediately toward Alex. I had so much compassion for him. We had been friends for ten years, and this shortcoming didn't eliminate the love I had and still have for him. There is purpose in everything, and deciding to lean into empathy and compassion developed tools that I still use today when it comes to forgiving. We often experience forgiveness when we need to receive it, but understanding what it takes to forgive helps us understand the weight of the forgiveness we've already received from Christ.

After discovering the relationship between Alex and my pastor, I was uncertain how to address the situation. Each day, I showed up as my usual self, guided by the grace of God, because I didn't sense He was telling me to leave immediately. Not feeling safe enough to share my pain, I made one of the most detrimental choices: I internalized everything. I kept it all inside. I replayed the pain endlessly without a proper outlet to express or process it, and that led me into a state of disassociation. It felt like the suffering was happening to someone else. Honestly, it felt like I was dying. My body couldn't endure the pain I had been bottling up. I lost an alarming amount of weight. I was like a mere shell of my former self.

During all this turmoil, I developed the intimacy with God that I had longed for. I started the year yearning for a deeper relationship with Him, and through this painful experience, He led me to that intimacy. Each day, I went to work, knowing what I knew, and had to adapt my life dramatically. I would start my mornings with worship, Bible reading, and prayer, pleading, "God, if You don't get me through this, I won't make it." Each day, it was the grace of God that carried me.

I immersed myself in the Bible, turned off secular music, avoided TV, and limited my social interactions. My routine became a cycle of quiet time with God, work, and barely surviving the day. Spiritually, I was awakening, yet in other ways I felt tormented and at the edge of despair. Though I wasn't contemplating ending my life, the pain made me feel like my life was coming to an end. I had reached a point where I could no longer internalize my emotions. My desperation became a cry: "God, I need You now!"

After a difficult conversation with my pastors and parents, we agreed that taking some time away was the best course of action. Little did I know, that time away would lead me to a crucial invitation to surrender.

My first stop was Kansas City, where I visited the International House of Prayer. I drove seven hours there, feeling so lost and broken that nothing seemed to offer relief. It was like I was drowning. I was ready to finally feel all the hurt, anger, and confusion I had been holding in and to surrender it all to God. My niece accompanied me, and I'm not typically emotional, so I warned her, "I'm going to cry when we get in there."

The worship and messages that day were exactly what I needed. In His presence, I released all the pent-up emotions. I remembered this verse: "In Your presence is fullness of joy" (Psalm 16:11, AMP). Even though I hadn't completely recovered, I believed I could regain my joy. I understood that God wasn't going to let this suffering be my end but, rather, He was revealing Himself to me through it.

After about a week in Kansas City, I took an impromptu trip to L.A. to visit my friend Randy. While there, I visited ONE L.A. church on Pentecost Sunday when Pastor Touré Roberts delivered a life-saving sermon called "When Everything Changed."*

* Touré Roberts, "When Everything Changed" (sermon, One: A Potter's House Church, Los Angeles, Calif., May 20, 2018), youtube.com/watch?v=Bn28AQL2Zno.

He spoke on Acts 2, about the disciples waiting for the Holy Spirit's outpouring. They likely waited in a state of sadness and hopelessness after Jesus ascended to heaven, yet though His departure devastated them, it was part of God's great plan to bless them with the Holy Spirit and send them out to the nations. That sermon marked a turning point for me, helping me understand that although my current situation was painful, it had a purpose.

During the service, a weight lifted off me. The journey didn't become easier afterward, but I regained my fighting spirit. I stayed in L.A. for two weeks, attended a creative conference at Universal Studios, and rediscovered my genuine smile. I posted a quote attributed to Maya Angelou—"Nothing can dim the light that shines from within"—feeling that I wouldn't succumb to the pain. I sensed God's presence with me throughout that trip, affirming that He was saving my life.

I returned to Chicago, but things didn't return to normal. I resigned from my staff position but continued to serve as a volunteer until God released me, which took time. Sometimes He requires us to surrender even when it's painful to do so and doesn't seem to benefit us. Forgiving those who hurt us is a big part of surrendering unconditionally to Christ. It's in these times of hardship that God develops our capacity to love with His heart rather than our own. Can we still obey and let painful things go even when those who hurt us don't acknowledge their wrongs?

I don't have a neatly tied-up conclusion for you. I moved to L.A. in August of that year, and as far as I know, everyone in

Chicago moved on with their lives. For me, the resolution lies in having forgiven and embraced God's heart for His people. Sometimes our journey with God involves a yes whose fruit we won't see until He deems the time right. I'm confident that the life I live today and the favor I experience are the results of how I handled the unexpected pain and betrayal I faced. Trusting God is one thing, but knowing that God trusts you is a profound experience. God used my darkest times to reveal my true purpose. It was hard and at times felt unbearable, but God knew I could handle it. He trusted me with that pain and the journey of forgiveness, leading me closer to His heart.

As I reflect on this journey, I'm reminded that life often unfolds in ways we can't predict. Expecting the unexpected becomes essential when we surrender our plans to Christ. He invites us to trust Him not only with our yeses but also with our uncertainties and fears. Embracing this journey means acknowledging that His ways are higher than ours and that often the path He has for us is filled with twists and turns that lead to greater growth and deeper intimacy with Him. When we surrender our journey to Christ, we open ourselves to the possibility of miraculous transformations, both in ourselves and in the lives of others. Every challenge we face, every sacrifice we make, and every unexpected detour can become a sacred opportunity for God to work through us, shaping us into vessels of His love and purpose. In surrendering to Him, we discover that our journey isn't just about us—it's about fulfilling His greater plan, where the unexpected becomes a testament to His faithfulness and grace.

Every challenge we face, every sacrifice we make, and every unexpected detour can become a sacred opportunity for God to work through us, shaping us into vessels of His love and purpose.

Pause + Reflect

For the enemy to come after me at that level and with that much intensity highlights his insight into who God was leading me to become. The same is true for you: The level at which the enemy attacks you is a revelation of the power that God has placed inside you. It's a revelation of who God has called you to be. The enemy isn't out here attacking people who won't make moves for the kingdom. His desire is to hit you so hard that you give up before you say yes.

Your current season of suffering could also be God's way of pursuing you. Maybe what you are experiencing has a reason that will be clear only once you invite God into it. No matter how messy it feels, let Him into your journey. He is already in the midst of your pain, working things together for good (Romans 8:28). Here are a few questions to sit with:

Your current season of suffering could also be God's way of pursuing you.

1. Why did this painful season happen?

2. Who is God inviting you to become?

3. What does it look like to do life with God in the midst of this pain?

4. What are you discovering as a result of this journey through the unexpected?

5

Finding Confidence in Your Yes

Moses protested to God, "Who am I to appear before Pharaoh? Who am I to lead the people of Israel out of Egypt?"

—Exodus 3:11

The more we grow in our relationship with Jesus, the more we discover who we really are. That process of discovery becomes a journey of its own. We start to see ourselves the way God does. Seasons of revealing are when we experience God as Abba, our Father. He takes His time walking us through how He created us. We have to accept what He thinks and says about us while we remove the labels that life has attached to us. It's almost as if we discover how much God chooses us in our choosing Him. Our obedience is linked to becoming the person He created us to be. There are things about myself that I would have never discovered had I not taken steps of obedience into environments that called new things out of me.

I still remember how I felt the first time I ever preached a sermon. As you may recall, in 2021, I joined the staff at Centerpoint Church, a Free Methodist, predominantly Caucasian church located in a fairly conservative town. It was far from the typical setting where one might expect my preaching ministry to begin. Although my presence was quite different from the norm there, I was always warmly embraced by my Centerpoint family. I never felt merely tolerated as one of the few people of color on staff; instead, I felt genuinely loved and accepted.

Though my role was behind the scenes, Pastor John saw something in me. He asked me to preach, and admittedly, I was initially overwhelmed by the environment. I began to second-guess myself, wondering about everyone's expectations and whether I would meet them. I was very comfortable with my own style—I had shaved designs on the sides of my head, with blond and brown braids tied up in a bun, and I wore a blazer with sneakers and large hoop earrings. But I worried that people might see me and decide to walk out.

I prayed, feeling out of place and unsure, "God, I'm just this loud girl from the west side of Chicago with a background in production; I don't belong up here." Honestly, I didn't even know what it meant to preach—I had no understanding of exegesis or hermeneutics.

But I had everything I needed: a personal relationship with Jesus and an understanding of what He was teaching me in that season. That turned out to be more than enough. Have you ever had an experience when everything you've known and endured suddenly becomes the foundation for an unexpected breakthrough? When you realize that every place God leads you, He also equips you for, you find a confidence that transcends your own abilities. That's how I felt when I stepped onto the stage.

I shared with the congregation what God had been revealing to me, and I invited them into the journey with me. God showed up in a way that I had never experienced before. I watched Him bring Scripture alive, not just for those listening, but for me as well. I saw things in the passage that I hadn't noticed before.

I often say that preaching is where I'm most intensely surrendered. It feels like an out-of-body experience where I completely yield to what God wants to do. If I were to step onto that platform with full control rather than full surrender, I would falter every time. There's no way I could find the words or strength to speak without God. When I preach, I get to experience afresh the purpose of the Holy Spirit's gift—empowering us to do things we otherwise couldn't.

Your Yes Qualifies You

Before I stepped onto the stage, the real challenge for me was not delivering the sermon but accepting that I was worthy of the opportunity. At that time, I had no formal training or background that prepared me to preach. I knew nothing about seminary, and I hadn't followed the typical path to becoming a preacher. I'm sure I wasn't alone in wondering how I ended up behind the pulpit. I was simply living out a moment that was born from steps of obedience. Surrendering to God often leads to opportunities for which you feel unqualified, yet it also enables you to exceed any preparation you could have imagined. God doesn't call us into things where He hasn't already prepared the way.

Sometimes it feels like the life I now live is so different from what I expected. But if I'm truly honest, I can see the thread of God's plan woven through the journey.

In 2014, I was living in Chicago after deciding not to move to L.A. upon completing graduate school. I got involved at my local church, and soon after, they asked me to lead a young adult ministry. What began as a simple gathering of like-minded young adults quickly grew into something more. What started as a small group of ten people blossomed into a weekly gathering of a hundred.

At the time, leading the ministry felt like I was just saying yes to God and to my pastor. But God was laying the foundation for my calling. He was nurturing a gift within me that He would later call me to wholeheartedly embrace. He was preparing the way.

Fast-forward to 2020. After I had been in L.A. for two years, the pandemic hit, throwing us all into the unknown. At the start of it, my best friend, Stephanie, felt led by God to fast for twenty-one days, and she invited me to join her. At that point, the painful experience of Alex cheating on me had left me just a shell of my former self. I was more reserved and hesitant to let new people into my life. It wasn't that I didn't want to make friends, but I was scared of exposing my heart to the kind of hurt I had experienced before. I wasn't sure what the fast would lead to, but I chose to say yes.

Stephanie, another friend, and I prayed every morning at five-thirty. Each day, God used our prayer time to chip away at the shell I had become comfortable living within. Although there was safety in my timidity, I discovered a beautiful freedom as I began to entrust specific areas of my life back to God. I thought I was saying yes to a fast, but God used that yes to restore my heart. I was delivered from the pain that had silenced my voice and made me think it wasn't needed.

When we are contemplating an act of obedience, we can often allow the outcome to be our highest motivating factor. I was fixated on the fast itself at first, but God was working deep healing in me during the whole experience. While the outcome is important to consider, the hope is that as we progress in our relationship with the Lord, we decide to say yes even when we have no idea where it's leading. Our motive in surrendering must be to please God—nothing more and nothing less. Because, in life, there is always a possibility that the fruit of today's yes may not unfold until several years from now. If that were the case, would you still say yes?

While the outcome is important to consider, the hope is that as we progress in our relationship with the Lord we decide to say yes even when we have no idea where it's leading.

God Wants Your Heart

I'm always amazed when I realize that God isn't really after the things He asks us to leave behind. What He's truly after is our hearts and seeing His plans for our lives come to pass.

That twenty-one-day fast turned out to be the beginning I never could have imagined. Through it, I found the boldness to reconnect with the creative side of myself that I had buried with my broken heart. It may sound dramatic, but when you've had your heart broken, you tend to avoid everything that reminds you of the person you're trying to forget. For me, creating, sharing the Word, leading others, and even watching certain TV shows all became reminders of a life I no longer wanted any part of. But by the end of the fast, I was able to separate my pain from my passions and rediscover my purpose.

During the fast, I kept joking about wanting to start a podcast. The funny thing is, I had no idea what starting a podcast would actually involve. My initial plan was to take some old vlogs I made when I moved to L.A., convert them into audio, and build from there. Since I've always lived at the intersection of faith and culture, I thought the podcast would revolve around discussing similar topics. But God had other plans.

I'll never forget when my best friend called me after her prayer time. She told me I needed to take seriously what God was asking me to do. Until then, I had thought the podcast was just my idea, a creative venture. I had no idea it was an assignment from heaven. Taking her words to heart, I went straight to Best Buy and bought a microphone.

I researched everything I could about podcasting, and I began praying about it earnestly. It became clear that this podcast wasn't just my project; it was God's. I realized I couldn't build it on my own. It needed to start with Him and His purpose. So, I asked Him what He wanted me to do.

Honestly, when He revealed His vision and instructions for the first episode, I was overwhelmed. He was asking me to share the story of how Alex had cheated on me with someone who played a significant role in my growth as a leader. I carried this story with a heavy sense of shame. I hadn't even told it to those closest to me. The idea of exposing my most painful and vulnerable experience to the world felt daunting, even humiliating.

Yet God was working to address the shame I felt and highlight the power of my story. He wanted me to trust Him and share my story—even though it seemed like an awkward start to a podcast—so I could begin to heal.

I knew that once I went public with my testimony, there would be no going back. Something I had intended to keep private forever would be out there for everyone to hear. I didn't feel ready to share it until I realized the focus of my story was not what had been done to me but the God I had met while navigating that pain. God was asking me to introduce Him to others in the same profound way I had encountered Him.

He wanted to reveal how He came to me in my suffering so others could see they could meet Him in their own struggles. Now the podcast was no longer just about me; it was about disrupting my comfort to help others experience Him. I didn't realize at the time that this would also bring to light deep, hidden areas of pain I had left untouched. God's love for me was so great that He used this assignment to lead others to healing, all while guiding me through my own. As hard as it was to share my experience, I followed the guidance of Revelation 12:11:

> They overcame and conquered him because of the blood of the Lamb and because of the word of their testimony, for they did not love their life and renounce their faith even when faced with death. (AMP)

God's love for me was so great that He used this assignment to lead others to healing, all while guiding me through my own.

Let Faith Lead

I launched *Life in Perspective* in April 2020, and my life has never been the same. The podcast became the place where God began to cultivate my teaching gift, which He profoundly revealed to me the following year.

Just three months after launching the podcast, I was invited to speak on a panel of remarkable women at a conference hosted by Pastor Sarah Jakes Roberts. To say I was terrified would be an understatement. When I got the call, I was convinced they had the wrong number—it had to be a mistake. I kept questioning what qualifications I had to sit on a panel with doctors, pastors, prolific speakers, and influencers. These women had been ministering and working for years, and here I was, a girl with a podcast, suddenly invited to share space with them.

After the panel, I felt like I had tanked. In my mind, I could have done so much better. I was trapped in my own head, as I often am when I feel an opportunity is too big for me. I was so focused on not messing up that I didn't allow myself to be entirely present. I didn't let the version of Brenda who had been invited show up as her true self. I was there, but I wasn't owning the moment, and I didn't let God shine through me, because I was overthinking every detail.

Did God still use that opportunity and my words? Absolutely. But I can't help wondering how much more He could have done if I had let faith lead instead of fear. This is what I mean when I say that the journey of saying yes doesn't just lead to new opportunities; it leads to discovering more about who God is. I wasn't on the panel by accident. I was there because God had a purpose for me. Through this experience, I've embraced that He doesn't call the qualified; He qualifies the called. Where my abilities end, His begin, and I can trust Him to always fill the gap. When we say yes to God, He doesn't expect us to rely on our own strength or qualifications. Instead, He equips and qualifies us for every step of the journey. God's calling comes with His empowerment. He provides the wisdom, resources, and strength we need to fulfill the purpose He's placed before us.

The more we understand His character, the more we can trust that He won't leave us on our own when life feels overwhelming. Each step we take in faith allows us to see His faithfulness in action. He's the one who is always covering our weaknesses with His strength and guiding us through situations that might otherwise feel impossible. Saying yes to Him is saying yes to transformation, growth, and the privilege of seeing His power work through our lives in ways we never imagined.

My entire faith journey has been marked by choosing to stand boldly in the face of feeling inadequate. Time and again, I find myself telling God, "This is crazy; I have no idea how we got here, but I'm going to keep saying yes because I trust You." And every time, He shows up in the most unexpected ways. I surrender to the truth that if God leads us to a specific place, it's because He has something for us to do there. The weight of that moment is on Him, not on me and not on you. When we place the outcome in His hands, it always aligns with His plan.

When we feel like we're in over our heads, God is teaching us to rely completely on Him. That dependence is strongest when every form of self-reliance is stripped away. He becomes our only source of help, and it turns out He's the best option. Often, when we doubt our ability, it's because we're measuring the task against our own capacity instead of the power of the One who lives within us. Our weakness is simply an opportunity for a miracle, a perfect opportunity for His glory to be revealed in and through us. Like Paul wrote,

[The Lord] said, "My grace is all you need. My power works best in weakness." So now I am glad to boast about my weaknesses, so that the power of Christ can work through me. (2 Corinthians 12:9)

Our weakness is simply an opportunity for a miracle, a perfect opportunity for His glory to be revealed in and through us.

Embarking on the journey of yes means following the path of grace. One of the most encouraging things I've heard God say is "I know you feel like you don't have enough to do what I'm asking, but all you need is My grace." That's why it's so important to say yes to God's calling, even when you feel more comfortable staying where you are. When God asks for our yes, He's promising that His grace will empower us to do things we never thought possible.

What Is in Your Hand?

God always amazes me with what He draws out of me. I often find myself saying, "I didn't know I had that in me" or "I didn't know I was holding that in my hands."

No matter how many times I've seen God show up and prove Himself faithful, I can still struggle to accept that He's constantly asking me to step into things that feel far beyond my own abilities. Preaching, podcasting, and leading Bible studies are just a few examples of things that make me ask, "God, are You sure You want me to do this?" But the more I say yes, the more confident I become—not in myself, but in God's ability to work through me. Even when my yes to God requires me to say no to something I want, I choose to trust Him and follow His lead.

In 2023, after I quit my job, God began opening doors to some incredible opportunities. I was amazed at the platforms He was giving me access to. In June of that year, I was offered the chance to produce a women's event for a large platform. I was thrilled—it felt like a dream to do something I loved while serving a ministry that had been so pivotal in my faith journey.

As we began planning, I was in a meeting, discussing topics for the speakers, and during that call, I felt God whisper, "Elijah and the widow." I jotted it down, not thinking much of it at the time. I figured it was something to suggest for one of the other speakers.

But as the planning progressed, something didn't feel right. By the second meeting, I felt unsettled, like maybe this wasn't where I was supposed to be. And the truth was, I needed the money from this job. I wasn't working full time, and my income wasn't consistent. So when I sensed God telling me this wasn't what I should be doing, I was shocked. But I chose to trust Him and said no to the producing opportunity. I knew if He was asking me to walk away, He had something better in store.

In seasons of waiting and transition, it's crucial to consult God about everything, even opportunities that seem like they come from Him. Pausing and asking, "Is this what You desire for me right now?" is never a bad choice.

A month later, just two days before the event was set to happen, I was in Zara, one of my favorite stores, when my phone rang. It was an invitation to preach at the very event I'd turned down the opportunity to produce. I couldn't help but laugh and say, "God, You play too much." Without hesitation, I said yes, feeling an unexpected confidence, as though I'd been preparing for this all along. The only thing I worried about was how I was going to do my hair, since I had to cancel my hair appointment to fly to Dallas in time for the event.

God had already orchestrated everything. That whisper during the planning call—"Elijah and the widow"? That was the sermon He wanted me to preach. I spent the next two days trying to change the passage to something more familiar, but God made it clear that this was the assignment.

What I haven't mentioned yet is that the place I was going to preach was the Potter's House of Dallas. If you don't know, preaching at that church is like performing at Madison Square Garden. It's a church with a deep history and one of the largest congregations in the country. To preach there was a dream I never dared to dream.

Yet, despite the significance of the opportunity, the platform itself wasn't what weighed on me. It was the responsibility of being a vessel of God's transforming power for the women He had led to that room. As I walked from my seat to the pulpit, more nervous than I could express, I had no notes—

just the text. But something shifted inside me. The nerves that had made me shrink during that panel three years earlier had no power over me now. I leaned completely into God's strength, and the anointing did what only it can do.

I experienced a boldness I'd never had before, and I knew the Holy Spirit was leading me, providing the exact wisdom and words that were needed. That sermon didn't just affect those listening—it changed my life. God ministered to me even as He used me to minister to others.

I understood a valuable lesson that day: Stop looking for validation from the room. If I wait for the room to confirm I belong, I limit what God wants to do through me. I can see now that I belonged on that stage—not because of my own merit, but because, as God's vessel, there was something unique that only I could share with the attendees.

The same is true of you. The partnership between you and God brings something good and unique to the world. If God leads you to it, He will lead you through it. Trusting Him is where you find the strength to continue saying yes.

My decision to trust God and say no to an opportunity that seemed right led me into a yes that firmly established me in my calling. And in the end, that's what mattered most to God.

Your Yes Answers Prayers

Let's be real, though. The more confidence we find in saying yes to God and the more our yes leads us into opportunities, the easier it is to assume that every open door we are presented is for us. That couldn't be further from the truth. Our yes is always connected to the lives of others. We must look to live as vessels waiting to be poured out, not so much filled up. With that perspective, our posture becomes "God, what can I do for You? How can my life serve Your mission?" This humble surrender keeps us from being self-focused. We have to stop giving God a yes, looking for what He will do for us. Obedience isn't a transaction; it isn't a trade.

Los Angeles, often called the City of Dreams, lives up to its reputation. It's more than just a theme in movies and TV shows; it's the reality for many people here. Most residents come with dreams of making it big in Hollywood, whether as actors, as artists, or behind the scenes in production. Moving to L.A. should have been all about making connections and advancing my career. But I decided to shift my focus when I received a revelation from God's Word:

Seek the Kingdom of God above all else, and live righteously, and he will give you everything you need. (Matthew 6:33)

This verse became my mantra and a real game changer for me. Instead of chasing my dreams first, I chose to pursue God and let my dreams follow if that was His plan, even if I felt inadequate. By placing God first and following His leading, I've learned that when He offers me a chance to say yes, I'm often answering the prayers of those who are crying out to Him. The countless women who needed courage to trust God in the journey were uplifted by my podcast. The man who was an atheist felt seen and loved and chose to follow Jesus after hearing my sermon at church. In these spaces where I felt unqualified, undeserving, God was using my obedience to speak to His children.

So, when you're wavering, contemplating what you might lose and whether your yes is worth it, remember that your response to God could be the answer to someone's prayers. It might feel daunting, but His grace is more than sufficient to equip you for the path He's calling you to.

I've always been moved by Moses's encounter with God, where he listed all the things he felt he lacked. He confronted his fears and feelings of inadequacy. The truth is, everything Moses needed was already in his hands; he just needed to surrender it to God and let Him accomplish His will by working His supernatural power through Moses's ordinary efforts. All God asked of Moses was a willing yes.

Moses pleaded with the LORD, "O Lord, I'm not very good with words. I never have been, and I'm not now, even though you have spoken to me. I get tongue-tied, and my words get tangled."

Then the LORD asked Moses, "Who makes a person's mouth? Who decides whether people speak or do not speak, hear or do not hear, see or do not see? Is it not I, the LORD? Now go! I will be with you as you speak, and I will instruct you in what to say."

But Moses again pleaded, "Lord, please! Send anyone else."

Then the LORD became angry with Moses. "All right," he said. "What about your brother, Aaron the Levite? I know he speaks well. And look! He is on his way to meet you now. He will be delighted to see you. Talk to him, and put the words in his mouth. I will be with both of you as you speak, and I will instruct you both in what to do. Aaron will be your spokesman to the people. He will be your mouthpiece, and you will stand in the place of God for him, telling him what to say. And take your shepherd's staff with you, and use it to perform the miraculous signs I have shown you." (Exodus 4:10–17)

I always feel so seen when I read this story, because I can replace Moses's name with mine and see the same conversation I'm consistently having with the Lord. I'm always trying to prove to God that I'm the one He doesn't want to use: "Lord, pick anyone but me." Can you relate? Yet when Moses gave this excuse in the passage above, God proved how He would use the very thing Moses thought made him unworthy. That says a lot about how God sees us. Nothing is ever wasted in His hands. The things you see as reasons God can't use you are the very things He wants to use for His glory. "Oh, you stutter? Great. I'm going to send you to speak on My behalf." God uses our weaknesses to fulfill His will. And over time, as we say yes, God reveals ourselves to us. We start to adopt His perspective of us. The yes God is asking us for is always to lead us into better.

Despite his fear, Moses chose to say yes to God. He stood before Pharaoh and boldly demanded, "Let my people go" (Exodus 5:1). God used Moses's obedience to answer His people's prayers and deliver them. I often wonder what would have happened if Moses had chosen to disobey. How different would his life have been?

What we need to understand is that our disobedience doesn't stop God's plan—it just changes our role in it. God's purposes always prevail. Even if Moses had said no, God still would have delivered the Israelites from Pharaoh's rule. That was always the plan. But who would Moses have been? He would have missed out on discovering the leader, prophet, and intercessor that God had designed him to be. He would have never realized the strength, resilience, and authority that were within him, waiting to be unlocked through obedience.

More importantly, he would have never known God intimately as a guide, provider, and protector. During his journey, Moses came to know God's faithfulness as He led the Israelites through the wilderness, His provision when manna fell from heaven, and His protection in times of danger. Without stepping into his calling, Moses would have missed out on a life marked by purpose, miracles, and a profound relationship with the One who chose him.

In the same way, when we say yes to God's calling, we're not just completing a task—we're stepping into the fullness of who He created us to be, experiencing Him in ways we couldn't otherwise. It's not only about the destination; it's about the transformation that happens in us along the way.

When you're wrestling with whether or not to say yes to God's call, it's worth asking yourself, *Who do I miss becoming if I don't obey?*

Pause + Reflect

Have you missed out saying yes to God because of your low view of self? Have you missed or fumbled the things He had planned for you because you felt unworthy, unqualified, or unprepared? Take heart. God isn't making you trial-and-error your way into His purpose. He isn't playing chess with your life. Instead, He is preparing a path that will lead you right where He always intended for you to be.

Although I grew up a pastor's kid and tried to run as far as I could from ministry, I became a preacher. Looking back, I can easily see how my journey led me right into what I had been running from my entire life. Every yes was an opportunity to allow God to cultivate the gifts He placed inside me so that in due season the world would reap the harvest of my yes.

Now, what about you? What is God asking of you in this season? It's easy to focus on reasons you can't do something, but this time, consider why you can. Perhaps everything leading up to this point has been preparing you and equipping you with all the tools you need to move forward.

Just as Moses initially responded to God's call with a strong no, you too might find yourself hesitating. Yet God is ready to use what you already have to fulfill His purpose.

1. What are things in your life that make you feel unworthy of God's call?

2. What is in your hand? What has God given you that has prepared you for the journey you are currently embarking on?

3. What group of people do you sense God has created you to be an answer for?

4. What is the first or next step you can take toward the calling you feel unqualified for?

All these questions will lead you closer to surrendering your yes. Even more than that, when you acknowledge where you feel unworthy, you invite God into those spaces to provide you with the truth about yourself according to Him.

6

Trusting God in the Uncertainty

Jesus responded, "Why are you afraid? You have so little
faith!" Then he got up and rebuked the wind and waves,
and suddenly there was a great calm.
—Matthew 8:26

Scripture tells us, "The LORD is close to the brokenhearted"
(Psalm 34:18, NIV). It's a statement that often feels ironic
because if we let them, the pains and disappointments of our
journey can feed us the lie that God has left us when we need
Him the most. Yet, in chapter 4, I shared how I developed an
actual relationship with Jesus during one of the most devastating periods of my life. What I didn't know during that season is that darker times were still to come and I was going to
need God more than ever.

For a while, I worked to get back to the Brenda before the
heartbreak. I was trying my best to put the pieces of my life
back together. But after I moved to L.A. in 2018, the progress I
had made completely unraveled. I was so hurt and broken that
I retreated within myself. I was a shell. I had no desire to make
friends, create, or do anything else that would serve as a reminder of the betrayal I had just weathered.

Unfortunately, reminders were everywhere. Meeting new people felt like I was opening myself up to the possibility of pain. Creating and producing content with friends reminded me of what I had lost when I moved. I knew I needed to be in church, so I attended, but I didn't engage in it the way I used to. I would hear the Word and leave right away, not wanting anyone to see me or know me. I was hiding in plain sight.

After the fallout with Alex, I had carefully packed my whole life into a box and thought it was secure. When I moved to L.A., the bottom suddenly fell apart, and everything scattered on the ground. Those first weeks in L.A., I tried to tape the box back together and find all the pieces of my life again.

Eventually, I realized God was giving me a new box, one that He was holding together, filled with new items, and He was giving me new people to help carry the load. The issue was that I was so broken I didn't think I could trust what God was trying to give me. I struggled with understanding how He allowed something so devastating to happen to me in a place He had led me to. I didn't know how I could ever trust His instruction again. I had to rebuild my trust in God so that I could be open enough to receive what He wanted to give me.

Hard Questions Lead to Trust

You would think that—after growing up in church, years of ministry work, and intentionally growing closer to Jesus—I would have found it easy to trust God on a deeper level. I did not. It was really hard. Throughout all those hours and years at church, I couldn't recall anyone telling us that we could be honest with God about our feelings, especially the negative ones about faith or even God Himself. The message was to ask God questions meant we lacked faith. I was taught that because God is in control, everything happened the way He intended and we just needed to deal with it and trust Him. But I had gotten to a point where that no longer worked for me. I had questions, and since I was unable to ask them, God was turning out to be the villain in my story. I know now that we don't make it to a place of radical obedience and bold faith without asking the hard questions.

One day, I sat on my friend's rooftop to read my Bible and journal. And I had the epiphany that there was no way I was all in with God. I couldn't be. I hadn't been honest.

It was much like when you're in a relationship and something breaks your trust. You both decide to move past it, but neither of you communicates the pain you experienced. You can't move on from what you don't address. It was the same for me and God. I had been slapping clichés on my wounds instead of allowing them to heal properly. I decided to let it out and let Him in.

You can't move on from what you don't address.

I broke down and shared with God that I felt like He had left me. I had put my heart on the line with people, and they trampled it, and He just let them do it and get away scot-free. I was angry that I had to be the one to start over and they carried on with their lives normally. I wasn't throwing these accusations at God because I didn't believe He loved me. It was the exact opposite. I knew He loved me, which is why I couldn't understand how He had allowed it all to happen. It didn't feel fair, and for so long I asked, "Why me? I was a virgin, saving myself for my husband. I sacrificed my dreams to stay and serve in full-time ministry. I thought I was doing everything right, so why this storm? Why me?"

Then God whispered, "Why not you?"

That is when I discovered my view of our relationship was skewed. I had somehow concluded that life with Christ meant roses and easy days. But that isn't what He promised. This truth became real for me: Following Jesus will cost us. Always.

Having this honest conversation became an invitation for God to show me where He had been all along. He had been there the entire time, waiting for me to invite Him into my heart so He could begin to put the pieces back together.

> Look! I stand at the door and knock. If you hear my voice and open the door, I will come in, and we will share a meal together as friends. (Revelation 3:20)

We often think our toughest times reveal God's absence when they actually reveal just how present He is. When I'm down and out in my darkest hour, I see how close He is. Because I don't make it to the other side without Jesus being in the darkness with me. There is no Brenda Palmer on Instagram, on the podcast, or in this book without the grace of God, which saved my life. Jesus pursued me repeatedly in more ways than one.

That day on the roof, God walked me through every moment and revealed how He had been present. I thought He was allowing pain to shatter me, but He was protecting me. Losing things hurt, especially when I thought those people would remain with me forever. But I began to see the protection that comes with exposure. I had been enamored with Alex and my pastor, but God saw their actions. By revealing the hidden truth, He showered me with His mercy. Looking back, I'm reminded of a line written by King David that we are often too familiar with:

> Surely goodness and mercy shall follow me
> All the days of my life;
> *And I will dwell in the house of the Lord*
> *Forever.* (Psalm 23:6, NKJV, emphasis added)

If God's goodness and mercy are following us all the days of our lives, we can trust that everything that happens is indeed a manifestation of His goodness and mercy pursuing us. It's important to recognize that, in difficult times, the challenges we face may not always seem positive, but God's removal of us from certain situations—especially when we're resistant to leaving—reflects His unfailing love.

Initially, I held on to the belief that everything that had happened was preordained by God and I had to simply accept it without question. However, I've come to see that trust in God involves recognizing His active role in my life, not just as a distant architect of my fate, but as a loving guide who desires my well-being. Trusting God means understanding that His plans may include difficult transitions but those transitions are ultimately for my benefit. It's a journey where I'm invited to relinquish my desire for control and instead embrace His leading, knowing that every step is an expression of His goodness, even if it doesn't always *feel* good.

God showed me how He was always present, but He also gently showed me the error of my ways. We prefer to blame everyone else when things go wrong, but I must own my part in the pain I experience. Let me be clear: The betrayal wasn't my fault. But I had to ask myself some deep questions. Honest ones. Was there ever a time when God provided me a way of escape and, for whatever reason, I didn't take it? Yes, there was.

In 2016, I had sensed that God was finally giving me the okay to move to L.A. I talked it over with my pastor at the time, prayed through it, and set the moving date for April 2017. But fear and a desire to be loyal to the ministry I was serving stopped me in my tracks. I didn't go. I stayed, and exactly one year later, my life took a turn.

I sat with the reality that I hadn't heeded God's first call to move. In hindsight, I wouldn't change one thing about the journey. I know God in a way I never would have without that pain in my life. But had I said yes, even when I was afraid, I would have avoided the heartbreak. Sometimes God's call for us to step out in bravery is also His act of protection. I need you to know that being obedient to God isn't something you want to waver on. He knows what is best for us, even when we feel like we know better. I want us all to develop a trust in God so that when He calls, we go running.

Being real with God gave me space to start to forgive not just the people I had hurt and who had hurt me but also myself. I had been blaming myself and carrying so much shame around my story. By the time I headed down from my friend's roof that day, I knew I could no longer keep God out of the dark places in my heart. I could and needed to trust He could handle it all. I promise you the same: God can handle all your stuff. He's waiting at the door of your heart, waiting on you to invite Him in.

His Pursuit Leads to Healing

After laying it all out with God, I wanted to step into the light at the end of the tunnel. But it didn't happen that way. While the talk with God gave me a new perspective on our relationship, I had been burying my pain and feelings deep because I just wanted to be over it. I wanted to be better; I didn't want my life to be affected by past pain anymore. I just wanted to be normal again. I wanted to love again, but every step forward would lead me into a trigger that would knock me ten steps backward.

By this point I had moved into a new place, and I was working freelance jobs, still looking for something solid. But I was on a mission to prove that the betrayal hadn't broken me. I was determined to boss up and show them that, yeah, I was hurt, but look how I bounced back. It's easy to try to measure our healing by our success. If I had found a new job and a nice apartment and got my life popping right away, I would have been able to hide my unhealed heart. In His mercy, the Lord didn't allow that, because my heart needed to heal and my worth couldn't be attached to my success.

But let me tell you, life was rough. I was living in a house with five girls who were basically strangers yet over time became my family. For the first time in my life, I was on government assistance. Food stamps, Medicaid—I was really starting from the bottom. For eight months in the City of Dreams, God stayed by my side, providing for me even as I struggled to get by.

On the first anniversary of my traumatic experience, I traveled to Atlanta to attend a conference for creatives. God knew I needed to be there because I was in a space where they doubled down on the importance of mental health. This was pre-2020 when it wasn't as culturally trendy to speak openly about needing or attending therapy. Where I grew up, you went to therapy only if something was really wrong with you. Add to that the trauma from my only therapy experience: Before moving to L.A., I had talked to a therapist. I felt like she opened me up and then just left me to deal with everything. I felt no resolve, no relief, and I wasn't given any resources or tools to work toward healing. I was instantly turned off from ever doing that again. This conference, the topic, and my presence there could have been only God-ordained.

At the conference, I ran into a pastor who is now one of my big brothers in the faith. We chatted, and for the first time I told someone outside my family about what happened to me. He gave me a hug and said how sorry he was over and over. I felt numb. I never wanted people to feel sorry for me or pity me. My pastor friend grabbed my shoulders and said, "Brenda, you need to talk to somebody. You can't keep holding that in."

I just nodded and said, "Yes, sir."

God put someone in my corner to nudge me back into counseling. While I wasn't ready yet, eventually I went back to therapy. My brother encouraged me to try again. He even signed me up, paid for it, and made sure I took the next step toward healing.

I also met up with another friend at the conference. I owned a nonprofit that ran a summer camp, and he had helped me out during the previous summer. We spent a lot of time together at the conference and spoke on the phone. I thought I was interested in him romantically. In hindsight, I recognize my interest for what it was: another coping mechanism. I didn't have a great job, but if I could find someone that was interested in me, then I could hide from my pain in a new relationship.

I shot my shot, knowing I was in no condition to be involved with anyone, and texted him. He rejected me in a sweet way. He was flattered but just wanted to build a friendship with me. I told him I understood, and I did. But still, his text pushed me into the darkest place I had ever been.

After receiving his text on a Sunday night, I went to sleep and didn't leave my bed for almost five days. I retreated inside myself. Today I know that the correct term for what was happening is *passive suicidal ideation*. I had given up. My body was present, but I felt I had nothing to live for. I had no job, I felt like no one loved me and no one was choosing me, and I was done choosing me as well.

But God. He was standing at the door of my heart and sent my now best friend, Nik West, to knock on my actual door. Nik was one of my roommates, and every day, she would ask me to come out. Some days I ignored her; other days I yelled and cursed at her. I just wanted to be left alone to die. Life was too hard. I had no fight in me. I felt like God had gone to sleep in the middle of a storm in my life, but He was proving He was there and had no intention of giving up and leaving me. Nik was knocking in person, and in my heart and in my spirit, I could hear God saying, "Don't die here." His gentle yet determined pursuit stood firm against the lie that I had nothing to live for.

Finally, on day five, out of my annoyance with Nik, I got out of bed. I didn't realize I had been there for days. I walked to my door and let Nik in. She asked if I wanted to come out and watch TV with her. That happens to be my love language. I said yes. That was the most sacred yes I've ever given. It saved my life.

We watched TV for a bit. Then she asked if I wanted to go and get ice cream, something we did often. I said yes again. After ice cream, Nik asked if I wanted to go walk around the lake in our neighborhood. I said yes again. We were walking for about three minutes before I just broke down and allowed myself to feel the pain I had been trying to escape for the last year.

I wanted to move on so bad, but I hadn't been present enough to my pain for God to totally deal with it. It had grown too heavy for me to carry. Nik's relentless mission to get me out of my room was God's way of saying, "Let Me hold it for you." I said yes. I decided, from that day on, to no longer hold on to anything that the Lord was offering to carry for me.

In our hyper-individualistic culture, we can feel less than or weak for acknowledging pain. But I want to correct that for us. Pain and suffering make us aware of our need for God. During this hardship, I discovered another layer of who God is. He gives us the space to experience the human emotions He created us with. He wants us to feel. He doesn't want us to remain or die in our emotions, though. He wants to be our healer and to use our emotions to lead us closer to Him. One of the Scripture passages that encourages me when I'm trying to navigate emotions is the story of Elijah in the wilderness.

Pain and suffering make us aware of our need for God.

Elijah was afraid and fled for his life. He went to Beersheba, a town in Judah, and he left his servant there. Then he went on alone into the wilderness, traveling all day. He sat down under a solitary broom tree and prayed that he might die. "I have had enough, LORD," he said. "Take my life, for I am no better than my ancestors who have already died."

Then he lay down and slept under the broom tree. But as he was sleeping, an angel touched him and told him, "Get up and eat!" He looked around and there beside his head was some bread baked on hot stones and a jar of water! So he ate and drank and lay down again.

Then the angel of the LORD came again and touched him

and said, "Get up and eat some more, or the journey ahead will be too much for you."

So he got up and ate and drank, and the food gave him enough strength to travel forty days and forty nights to Mount Sinai, the mountain of God. There he came to a cave, where he spent the night. (1 Kings 19:3–9)

Elijah had just experienced one of his most successful confrontations. At Elijah's call, God rained fire down from heaven, proving His sovereignty over the false god Baal (18:22–40). Then, again through Elijah, God fulfilled His promise to send rain to end a drought for a people that were pretty unfaithful. All this put a target on Elijah's back, and he felt overwhelmed and just wanted to end it all. I'm so encouraged by this because it helps to prove that our feelings, even when they are suicidal, aren't too much for God to handle. Elijah asked the Lord to take his life, and God met him where he was, in the thick of his emotions.

The Lord said to him, "What are you doing here, Elijah?"

Elijah replied, "I have zealously served the Lord God Almighty. But the people of Israel have broken their covenant with you, torn down your altars, and killed every one of your prophets. I am the only one left, and now they are trying to kill me, too."

"Go out and stand before me on the mountain," the Lord told him. And as Elijah stood there, the Lord passed by, and a mighty windstorm hit the mountain. It was such a terrible blast that the rocks were torn loose, but the Lord was not in the wind. After the wind there was an earthquake, but the LORD was not in the earthquake. And after the earthquake there was a fire, but the LORD was not in the fire. And after the fire there was the sound of a gentle whisper. (19:9–12)

In a gentle whisper, God revealed Elijah's next assignment, reminding him that there was still something worth living for. That's exactly what God did for me. Even though I felt like I was searching for a way out of life, God met me where I was. He used Nik to silence the lie that I was alone, that no one cared. The way God used her to pursue me as I was slipping away is the same way He continually pursues all of us. When we least expect Him to, God shows up, reminding us that He's been there all along. God never interacts with us from a distance; even in our darkest experiences, no place is outside His reach.

*God never interacts with us
from a distance.*

Nik was with me every step of the way, ensuring I became the version of Brenda that God had revealed to her. Just as He remains present in our lives, guiding us toward who we are meant to be, she never gave up on me. She embodied God's love, and that's why He led me to live in that house when I moved to L.A.

Two weeks after that walk around the lake, I applied, interviewed, and accepted an offer for a new job. It was a dream job too. I became an associate producer on a women's talk show, which moved me closer to who God was leading me to become. I also started therapy and began an intentional journey toward healing. I didn't want to just get past the pain anymore. I wanted to heal in a way that would display the power and glory of God. By the grace of God, I'm still here, and I didn't die there.

Maybe, like me, you've walked through seasons of doubt, struggle, and pain so deep they felt consuming. Yet, even in those times, God never stopped pursuing you. His love isn't deterred by your fears, your questions, or even the times you may have turned away. He's present in the thick of it all— whispering hope, extending grace, and waiting patiently for your heart to turn back to Him. Just as He carried me, step by step, toward healing and purpose, He's guiding you, too, even when you can't see it. His desire is not just to help you get past the hard times but to see you whole, to see you living in the fullness of who He created you to be.

Pause + Reflect

When I was crying my eyes out on the plane during my move from Chicago to Los Angeles, God made me a promise:

> We know that God causes everything to work together for the good of those who love God and are called according to his purpose for them. (Romans 8:28)

I found immense peace and encouragement in the idea that *everything* truly encompasses all aspects of our lives; nothing is excluded from that powerful word. While this part of my journey was undeniably dark, God used it all to work for my good, and He will do the same for you.

A friend once told me, "Sometimes God allows our hearts to break to remove the things that we don't need." The dark and painful experiences we endure serve a purpose—they reveal issues we didn't even realize were holding us back. It's essential to understand that God doesn't cause bad things to happen; rather, He can use those challenges to shape us and fulfill His ultimate plan for our lives. While our struggles still hurt, we can take comfort, knowing that God is there, transforming our pain into growth and resilience, guiding us toward a future filled with hope and purpose.

So as you pause and reflect on the questions below, know that God will cause all your heartbreak and disappointment to work together for your good since you love Him and are called according to His purpose.

1. What is hindering your ability to be completely honest with God?

2. What things in your life are you using to mask areas of pain that you don't want to face?

3. What area of your life do you need to let God into so He can work His healing?

4. Look at the area you identified in the last question. What is God speaking to you regarding that part of your life?

Don't rush this process. These are questions you may have to sit with over time and revisit repeatedly. Make space for God to enter the darkest parts of your heart and shed light. He will bring you the freedom you didn't know you needed.

7

Courage Beyond Fear

Fear not, for I am with you;
be not dismayed, for I am your God;
I will strengthen you, I will help you,
I will uphold you with my righteous right hand.
—Isaiah 41:10, ESV

It's funny that as I sit here writing this chapter, I'm thinking about the fact that I originally eliminated it. I felt like I didn't have enough to share on this topic. Then it was like God laughed at me and said, "Really, Brenda?" I sat and thought how real He was with that challenge. I'm struggling with the topic of failure right now. The truth is, I didn't want to write this chapter. I'm a little embarrassed to say how often I ask myself, *What if I fail?* And I also am probably a little ashamed of the number of times this question has hindered my ability to say yes.

The fear of failure cripples us. Underneath so many of the questions we ask before we say yes is the worry of failing. But if we don't get a handle on it, that fear will ruin what God has entrusted to us to steward.

As I'm navigating the journey of being a preacher, a podcaster, and now an author growing in influence daily, I toy with the question *What if I fail?* more often than not. I don't want to mess up. Like so many, I hate making mistakes. As a recovering perfectionist, the pressure to get everything right can feel debilitating, especially when I sense that so much is riding on my decisions.

I took a monthlong break from traveling to just focus on writing this book. That month was the hardest month I've had in a very long time. I was beyond asking myself, *What if I fail?* I was smack dab in the middle of feeling like a failure. I'm oftentimes hard on myself because, without the traditional pastoral journey or training, I don't really feel like I measure up to the expectations that come along with my profession. Even now, while in seminary, I struggle with the fear of failing, but I'm pushing through. God has surrounded me with an amazing group of women in my cohort who have uplifted and encouraged me. Even though I often feel unworthy of being in the company of these women, let alone building relationships with them, they have been my guiding light. God has been so gracious to put me in a space with women who have been doing what I'm just now stepping into for twelve years, sometimes forty years. This season is revealing God as Abba Father to me. I'm worrying about failing and being timid, and here God is, padding me with the support, the resources, and everything else I need to ensure that I don't fail.

And isn't that just like God? While we're caught up in worrying about failure or fearing we won't measure up, He has already anticipated our need. In His grace, He places the right people, the right words, and His promises in our path to re-mind us that we aren't walking this journey alone. Whether it's through the encouragement of others, the truth of Scripture, or a period of unexpected peace, God is constantly surround-ing us with what we need to strengthen our confidence and trust. So, I urge you to pause and look around your own life—where has God already provided the support, the encourage-ment, or the promise that will lift you up? Those sources of life and hope are often right before us, waiting to be recognized as the tangible evidence of God's love and provision, guiding us through every step.

> God is within her, she will not fall;
> God will help her at break of day. (Psalm 46:5, NIV)

In context, this verse is referencing the city of Jerusalem, but we can apply it to our lives as we follow God's lead. If God is in us and He's the one leading us and guiding us, we can't fail. I know it's really hard to embrace that truth when you feel like a failure or you feel incompetent. We have to know that He's a God that never fails and He won't fail us. He never has; He never will. When you can't grasp that reality, recall the times when you said yes and you didn't fail. Even the times when you got it wrong, the rich grace and mercy of God cov-ered it for you. He allows even your mistakes to work together for your good. That is a truth you can hold on to. It's a truth that will root you in who God is—an unfailing, loyal Father—and who He is calling you to be.

*If God is in us and He's the one
leading us and guiding us, we can't fail.*

We can spend a lifetime asking, *What if I fail?* But what if we don't? What if the thing God is asking us to step into is really Him creating an opportunity to prove to us that we're not failures? Preaching is one of the areas where I feel the least confident, yet God consistently uses those opportunities to affirm that I'm exactly where I'm meant to be.

There's a church I love—One Community Church, where one of my favorite Bible teachers, Jada Edwards, serves alongside her husband, Dr. Conway Edwards. She has been incredibly influential in how I communicate the gospel, so when I was invited to speak at their singles conference, I was excited. But when I saw that Dr. Tony Evans, a general in the faith and someone I deeply respect, was also preaching, I felt overwhelmed. It's one thing to speak at the same event, but I was scheduled to preach on the same night—me first, then Dr. Evans. The weight of that reality made me nervous beyond words.

As I prepared to preach, I prayed for the confidence only God could give me, knowing that my calling was not about impressing anyone but about stewarding what God had already ordained. I asked Him to help me focus on His purpose rather than my fear. And when the time came, I surrendered entirely, and once again, I found joy and freedom in delivering the message He gave me. Afterward, Dr. Tony Evans looked at me and said, "Thank you, Brenda, for sharing that with us. You are a gift to the body of Christ."

I'm grateful that I didn't let fear hold me back. Had I shrunk away, I wouldn't have witnessed God revealing another layer of who I am in Him. Preaching that night, I wasn't just delivering a message—I was speaking directly to a group that often feels overlooked in the church: singles. I was able to affirm that this season of life is valuable and not just a waiting period for marriage. God gave me the courage to stand firm, speak boldly, and be myself. I was reminded that while our validation comes from God alone, He sometimes uses others to affirm us.

Anchored in Trust

For so many of us, the fear of failure is holding back our yes. We allow our emotions to take control, and that doesn't lead to lasting or meaningful results. Our feelings are too unpredictable to guide our lives. While they shouldn't be in charge, our emotions can point us to our deeper need for God. Here's my challenge: So what if we fail? The God who called us never does. His plans are written in stone, and He never wavers. That truth should be enough to fuel our yes. That truth should convince us to say, "I'm going to surrender, but not to the fear. I'm choosing to believe in God. I'm choosing to believe what God says about me."

The moment we surrender and say yes, we already have the victory. The victory may not look the way we expect it to, but there is no failing in that. The whole goal in following Jesus is that we would step into all things synced in fellowship with

Him. Our emotions remind us to draw near to Him, to seek His presence and wisdom. The aim is to anchor ourselves in something unchanging, reliable, and secure—that foundation is God and God alone.

> *The aim is to anchor ourselves in something unchanging, reliable, and secure—that foundation is God and God alone.*

When our foundation is our unwavering God, then when He asks us to take a step that feels so outside anything we would ever do, it becomes the perfect opportunity to trust Him. It's an invitation to say, "God, I trust You. And I trust the version of me that You can see."

This reminds me of Esther, a Jewish girl who ended up in the palace with the favor of the Persian king. When presented with an opportunity to put her favor on the line and be the voice to save her people, Esther was probably thinking, *Y'all, I just got here, and I don't really have the authority to make this happen.* Not only that but she would also be risking her life to make this request, to ask the king to deliver the Jews.

She instructed him to say to Mordecai, "All the king's officials and the people of the royal provinces know that for any man or woman who approaches the king in the inner court without being summoned the king has but one law: that they be put to death unless the king extends the gold scepter to them and spares their lives. But thirty days have passed since I was called to go to the king."

When Esther's words were reported to Mordecai, he sent back this answer: ". . . If you remain silent at this time, relief and deliverance for the Jews will arise from another place, but you and your father's family will perish. And who knows but that you have come to your royal position for such a time as this?"

Then Esther sent this reply to Mordecai: "Go, gather together all the Jews who are in Susa, and fast for me. . . . When this is done, I will go to the king, even though it is against the law. And if I perish, I perish." (Esther 4:10–16, NIV)

Although Esther was afraid and although she was risking her life, she stepped beyond the fear that keeps so many of us stagnant and she said yes. This is the posture we should adopt. Remembering how God showed up for Esther, we can say, "God, if this kills my career, if this removes the position, if this alienates me from people that I care about, that I love dearly, I'll do it anyway. Even through failure, I'll follow You."

And just as God came through for Esther, He will come through for us. Esther's courageous yes not only saved her life but also spared the Jewish people from genocide. God worked through her obedience to bring about a miraculous deliverance. This same God is faithful to show up in our lives when we step out in trust and obedience.

*God is faithful to show up
in our lives when we step out
in trust and obedience.*

Progress, Not Perfection

I often wonder if, before Esther stepped up to help deliver her people, she asked herself, *What if I fail?* Maybe she felt a surge of insecurity, reminded of times when she didn't quite meet the expectations placed on her. Like Esther, I've had to confront the fear of failure and overcome the doubt that resurfaces whenever I face something new.

Back in 2020, during the height of the pandemic, while many were losing jobs, I found myself in a unique position where work opportunities actually increased because of the rise of virtual production. So I decided to start my own production company. That year was also an election year, and through a connection with a friend who works as a producer, I was recommended for a major opportunity—to serve as a creative producer for a five-episode digital series on Tidal called *The Main Thing*. The show focused on the importance of voting. The concept was to have conversations about politics but in a relaxed, informal cookout style, making it more approachable for people outside the political world. I was both thrilled and incredibly intimidated. Although I had experience in production, I had never led a project of such significance.

Though I felt the weight of the task, I crushed the interview because I understood the heart behind the show. But once the work began, I struggled with the fear of failure. I knew my role, but I often held back from stepping into it. I was surrounded by people with far more experience, and despite my expertise, I doubted myself. We successfully produced four of the five episodes before I caught COVID. I wasn't able to finish the series with them, and my confidence took another blow. Looking back, I realize I didn't own the opportunity or believe that I was meant to be there.

I didn't show up as the best version of myself, because I allowed my fear of failure to hold me back. Yet, in that "failure," I discovered something crucial—I needed to trust not just in my abilities but in the God who brought me there. The fear of failure often stems from feeling unequipped, but if God brings you to a place, He has already equipped you with everything you need to succeed. I realized that my hesitation wasn't just robbing me of opportunities—it was robbing the people around me of what God had placed in me.

The following year, I had another chance to produce a digital talk show, and two days before filming, the host contracted COVID. Faced with what seemed like an impossible situation, we pivoted, creating a successful production featuring the host's husband, who was releasing a book. We pulled it all together in less than twenty-four hours, and it worked out seamlessly. I walked into the room, knowing I belonged there, and it shifted everything for me. The crew and the host even commented on how they sensed a new confidence and grace in me, which made them trust me more.

What I want you to take from this is simple: If God has brought you into a space, it's because that space needs something that only you can offer. This is a lesson I embrace continually. At every level of life, I find that God uses experiences to consistently prove to me that I'm enough. It's not about perfection; it's about showing up as the person God has called you to be. So, I challenge you to look around at where you are right now. Are you holding back because you don't feel like you're enough? Are you waiting for someone to validate you when God has already placed you there? Erase that mindset, and trust that your presence in that room is by divine design. There's a purpose in your being there, and it's time to show up with the full confidence that God has equipped you for it.

Remember, the Bible tells us in Romans 8:19 that the whole earth is waiting for the revealing of the children of God. This means creation is waiting on you to step into who you are. Like David standing before Goliath, we are confident not in what we bring to the table but in the God who has empowered us to be there. Trust that the God who brought you through past battles is the same God who will equip you to face the giants ahead.

In our humanity, we are bound to make mistakes. Our merciful God makes space for that because He doesn't expect us to always get it right. We will stumble, and that's okay. What we need to understand is to be gracious with ourselves, understanding that we are human. I'm currently on this journey of being more gracious to myself. I tend to critique everything I do, often in ways that aren't healthy. It's not just in ministry, preaching, or career endeavors. Even when I get hurt by a friend, I'll beat myself up for not seeing the signs sooner. I'll blame myself for making a mistake that was inevitable because I'm human.

Even in our surrender to Christ and submission to the Holy Spirit, we must leave space for our humanity—the part of us that reminds us how much we need God. We are not God. We are made in His image, but we need Him in order to reflect that image. And here's the beautiful part: God isn't looking for perfection from us. He desires partnership. He wants us to live in a way that acknowledges, "I don't have it all together, but when I look at where I am now, I see how far I've come."

God's desire is not for us to perform flawlessly but to grow closer to Him. As we walk in relationship with Him, we become more of the person He created us to be. That's what God is truly after—a heart that's passionately pursuing Him step by step.

What If It Works Out?

With all our fear around failing, we first need to consider, *What does failure look like in following God? Is success tied to the outcome of my actions? Or is success tied to my obedience to God?*

It's the trick of the enemy that makes us believe our yes to Jesus puts the responsibility of success on us when it absolutely does not. My choice to say yes to a thing is me saying, "God, I don't know where this is going to lead me. I don't know what is going to be required of me, but I trust You enough that if You're leading me there, You're going to get me through it.

You're going to sustain me. You're going to build me. You're going to develop me. You're going to have me covered."

The only failure is not taking the step toward God. The outcome is on Him. So the real question is: Do we trust God enough to know that He doesn't fail? Even if we follow His path and it leads us to a mistake, a loss, a rerouting, it's not a failure. It's part of His good plan, even if it doesn't look or feel good to us.

But here's the truth I'm embracing: If we experience failure while following God's lead, it very well may not be a bad thing. Because when you fail, you learn to depend on God. When you fail, you take yourself out of the driver's seat and you get in the passenger seat, choosing to relinquish control and trust God.

We also have to take into account that we serve an all-knowing, omnipresent God. Since He's all knowing, He knows what's going to happen after you take the step. Since He's omnipresent, He's already in the future that He's asking you to step into. Are you willing to trust that He has you, that He'll protect you, that He's with you, and that even the mistakes are part of His plan?

After I left my job, I embarked on a missionary journey, leading pop-up gatherings called Come Alive—where we would come together in coffee shops or other intimate spaces across the country to worship, fellowship, and dive into God's Word. I remember when God finally directed me to host a Come Alive in L.A. I wasn't sure what to expect, but I set the date, secured the venue, and posted the flyer. Everything seemed to fall into place with God's favor guiding the way.

But, on the morning of the event, I woke up with just four dollars in my account. I still needed to cover several expenses—the balance for the venue and an unexpected fee for the audio engineer. I didn't have the money. I couldn't even buy gas to get to the venue, let alone buy food. Still, I stepped out in faith that God would provide. My dad got a notification about my situation and, feeling for me, sent a hundred dollars. I put gas in my car and grabbed some fruit to eat, leaving me with just twenty-five dollars to my name.

I remember thinking, *God isn't going to fail me.* I just knew, without a shadow of a doubt, that He wasn't going to call me into this and not come through.

You see, whenever God would provide me with an instruction to host a Bible study or another event, I would always say, "God, if You want me to do it, You have to provide for it." And sure enough, He would do just that. He had done it just the previous month in Atlanta.

I was on a plane heading back to L.A. when God said, "Host a Come Alive Atlanta."

Atlanta wasn't in my schedule or budget, though. I replied, "God, I don't live in Atlanta. I live in L.A., so what are You saying?" But I just kept hearing Him say, "Host a Come Alive Atlanta."

"Okay. I hear You," I said. "If You want me to host a Come Alive Atlanta, You have to provide for me."

As soon as the plane hit the tarmac and I took my phone off airplane mode, I had a text from my dad: "You have a check here for $1,000." It was a check from my old apartment, the return of my deposit. The funny thing was, I had moved out of that apartment in January and the check came in May. God's timing was at work. That was the provision I needed to carry out the vision. I bought a ticket to Atlanta, secured a venue, found someone to lead worship, and did the pop-up. The way God had shown up for my past need was proof that I could trust Him to show up for my present need, even though I had woken up with four dollars in my account. He was going to provide.

The day of Come Alive L.A., I proceeded like I had everything I needed. I was locked in, confident that it would all go God's way. I trusted that all the residual fees were totally covered, not even questioning what would happen if I didn't have the money by the end of the night. I was so secure in God coming through I almost didn't remember to allow space in the event for people to donate.

After we wrapped up the night, I gave the audio engineer what we had collected from the donations and asked, "Would you mind if I gave you $75?" I knew that was only half her rate, but I didn't think I would be able to afford much more.

She gave me a sincere look and said, "Yeah, that's fine."

"No, it's not," I said. "I can tell by your face it's not okay."

She said, "No, no, no, it's fine. I completely understand."

But I heard God say, "Give her the entire rate—$150."

I opened my phone, and in my account was the exact amount I needed to pay her the rest of her rate. *God, if I give her this, that's all the money going out of my account.*

As soon as I hit Send, double what I had paid the audio engineer appeared in my bank account. I don't know where it came from, but it was there, almost instantly. I was so shocked, I thought I had stolen from her. It was so crazy. Yet I was able to cover the remaining charges of the event in full. Sometimes obedience asks you to release what is in your hand, place it in God's hand, and watch Him do what only He can.

I went home that night and called a friend who was vacillating about following an instruction God had given them. I told them the entire story and then shared what I had discovered because of this yes: "You just have to jump beyond the fear and trust God." We often wrestle with the question "What if it doesn't work out?" But, friend, what if it does? And even if the outcome doesn't match your expectations, what if God uses it to work something deeper in you? In that case, it still worked out, just in a way you couldn't have imagined.

Sometimes the journeys we fear the most are the ones that end up having the greatest impact on our lives. When I reflect on my year of solely depending on God, I realize it brought to the surface something deeper—control issues I didn't even know I had. When I felt discouraged or upset or questioned God, it wasn't because He failed to show up or keep His promises. It was because I didn't like the discomfort of not knowing what the next step would be or where the next provision would come from.

This journey of saying yes to God wasn't just about walking away from stability. It was about truly depending on Him. The fear of failure often causes us to hold tightly to the very things God is asking us to release. True surrender, a real yes, is about letting go of control.

True surrender, a real yes, is about letting go of control.

I want you to reflect on the areas in your life where fear has held you back—those things you haven't stepped into because you're afraid of what might happen. I encourage you to trust God enough to step into that fear. Watch how He shows up. Watch how He proves to you that you're capable of doing what He's called you to do.

And yes, you might fail. Sometimes we will miss the mark. But even in our failures, God never fails.

Pause + Reflect

Now, let's go back to our question: *What if I fail?* So what? God doesn't. Where you end is where He begins. When you come up short is the perfect time for God to step in. He makes up the deficit. Stop allowing fear to cripple you and hinder you from moving toward God.

Take a minute and prayerfully consider these questions:

1. When you think of what God has called you to do, how are you afraid of failing?

2. What does success look like in following God's lead in your life?

3. How do you know you can trust God to reveal Himself in the deficit?

4. How might God be using your fear or uncertainty to strengthen your faith and reliance on Him?

I promise you, when you begin to trust God for real, the fear of failure will no longer bind you. This is true for you and for me. I can see how the fear of failure has hindered me in following God's lead. It's like I become a dam to my own productivity because my fear prevents me from moving freely with God. So, I'm challenging both of us to take a step closer every day to the thing God's asking us to do. We won't allow fear to be an option. Whenever fear comes up, we're going to apply faith and remember how God showed up for Esther and for us in the past. That's the challenge—we're going to let God move freely in our lives and watch Him blow our minds.

8

At the Point of No

Many are the plans in a person's heart,
but it is the LORD's purpose that prevails.
—Proverbs 19:21, NIV

No matter how many times we say yes and experience the blessings that come with it, saying no remains an option. To be completely transparent, I often feel tempted to say no, even after committing to a yes. Sometimes I've said no, and each choice—whether yes or no—brings its own results.

I think of toddlers learning to speak, especially how my nieces and nephews loved the word *no*. Even when they wanted to say yes, they would confidently say no, as if it was their default setting. Over time, as they grow and face the consequences of their no, they discover the weight of their decisions. The journey of saying yes to God is much the same.

Sometimes no can feel like the better option. I can't count how many times I've consciously told God no because the thing He was asking me to do didn't align with the plan I saw for my life. As long as I can remember, I was adamant about not wanting to do ministry. I grew up as a preacher's kid and saw both the joys and the struggles of ministry. I had deeply internalized what I witnessed my parents go through as pastors. When you do life in service to others, sometimes sacrifices you make come with heartache, especially from the very people you dedicate your life to serving.

I dreamed of working behind the scenes in entertainment, not in church leadership. Yet, around 2016, God began to stir my heart toward my calling. It was almost as if He decided that He had allowed me to play this game of hide-and-seek long enough and now He was ready to use me. Despite this, I resisted, insisting that being "just Brenda" was enough. I felt God's nudges, so I answered His call, but in my own way. I went full-time staff. I led creative arts and production, while serving in women's ministry and leading young adults. God had a pastoral calling on my life, but I wasn't ready to step into ministry beyond the capacity I was already serving in.

One normal Saturday, for the first time, I led our congregational prayer. God was shifting me from the background to the platform. He had shared with my leaders what He placed inside me, but I chose to deny it. I was running like a track star.

A turning point came when a mentor told me something profound: "God doesn't move beyond our will." Every time I said no to what God had spoken over my life, I was hindering His work through me. Though this insight didn't immediately stop me from resisting His call, I began to see the ripple effects of my choices. *If God is truly speaking ministry into my life and I keep resisting, I'm putting a limit on what He wants to accomplish.* That realization struck me deeply. It wasn't that I intended to be rebellious—I've just always been clear about not needing or seeking a title to follow God. But I hadn't considered that my response to His calling could hold back what He wanted to do both in and through me. My no didn't just affect me; it affected the lives God intended for me to touch, just as my yes opened doors for His purpose to unfold.

The ways we say no to God can vary. Sometimes it's a direct refusal, like Jonah's, that makes us run away. Other times we may say yes with our words, but our hearts aren't entirely committed, and that shows in our actions—like with David or Moses. I've experienced every version of no. From outright running away from what God was saying, to saying yes but then acting in ways that revealed I wasn't totally on board, making me just as disobedient. There's also the kind of no we give to please people instead of God, driven by fear of what might happen. That's never a wise choice. Not just because of the consequences, but because the very people we're trying to please might be the ones affected by the yes we're withholding.

> The very people we're trying to please might be the ones affected by the yes we're withholding.

Waiting for Our Yes

Though we might run away or outright say no, God has a way of pursuing us when we least expect it. When He begins to unfold our journey, He is guiding us to say yes—either to our calling or to the path that leads us there. Even in our disobedience, He creates a way for us to find our way back to Him.

Even in our disobedience,
He creates a way for us to find
our way back to Him.

By now, you've likely noticed a pattern: Each time I enter a fast, God reveals things I wasn't even searching for. In 2017, I started the year with a fast, hoping to grow closer to God. During this one, He uncovered things about me that I hadn't seen before. As a visual learner, God often speaks to me through visions, and this time I saw myself traveling the world, speaking on a stage, and gathering people. But I couldn't accept it—I thought it must be a dream. I didn't completely grasp that I was preaching in the vision. I saw glimpses of what I'm doing today, and it scared me. I felt unworthy of what God was showing me, and honestly, I didn't want the responsibility that came with it. We don't always realize that saying yes to God comes with sacrifice.

I knew what I'd have to give up, and I wasn't ready to make sacrifices. The truth is, I didn't want to change my life or make better decisions, knowing those choices would affect the people I'd be responsible for after saying yes to God. I was convinced He'd made a mistake.

I remember making a conscious decision to live however I wanted. I wanted God to see that I didn't care how He viewed me. Despite whatever potential He'd placed within me, I didn't believe I was the one He wanted.

When my best friend from college got married that February, I was set on proving to God that I wasn't fit for His plans. I fell back into old habits, thinking that would disqualify me. I attended the wedding and had a great time at the reception. Then the party began. I smoked weed with my college friends and indulged quite a bit. The drinks flowed, and we made videos, played cards, and reminisced about our college days. We were living out our best adult version of college life while reflecting on all the good times. I was so high that I ended up in the back seat of my car, searching for snacks I knew weren't there, because I had the munchies. I did all the things. I was determined to show the God who knows everything that He'd made a mistake in calling me.

After returning home to my routine, I felt deeply convicted. While I had tried to show God my true nature, He ended up revealing it to me. I was no longer the Brenda who would behave like that, who would choose to party for days on end—it just wasn't who I was anymore. God reminded me that, despite my attempts to run, He still had a plan for me and wasn't changing His mind. Even when we say no, God remains faithful and waits for us to return.

That experience made me want to pursue God more deeply so I could truly understand how He sees me. I found myself asking, "Who is this version of Brenda that makes You so relentless in calling me, even when I resist with my entire being?"

I wanted to become that person, spurred on by the love that never stops pursuing. The only way to do that is by building a relationship with Him. It wasn't perfect, and at first, it was messy. But the more I said yes, the more I grew in my relationship with God, and the more I developed the trust to keep saying yes.

I want to encourage you because I know how hard it is to trust what God says about you and step into the unknown. Now that I'm walking in my purpose, I sometimes catch myself thinking, *I wish I had said yes sooner—who knows where I'd be now?* But God knew all along. My earlier nos only revealed that I wasn't ready to handle what He had prepared for me. Saying no gave God the opportunity to work on the broken areas of my life, areas that could have derailed my destiny if I had stepped in unprepared.

Despite God consistently showing me that I'm exactly who He's called for this purpose, I still wrestle with feelings of unworthiness. My life often is so far beyond anything I ever imagined that it's difficult to feel deserving. I've known people who, from a young age, always dreamed of being pastors, evangelists, or influencers—but that was never me. Yet somehow God led me right to where I was meant to be, whether I expected it or not.

Maybe you've felt this before—that sensation when God brings you into opportunities that seem too good to be true. Perhaps you believe you're unworthy of the favor and calling God has placed on your life. Or maybe you envisioned a different career path for yourself. Wherever you are in your journey of yes, remember that your life follows God's plans, not your own. Even your mistakes can guide you toward the destiny He's designed for you.

As surprising as it is to see where I've ended up, I know this was part of His plan all along. The more I embrace that truth, the more I realize that no is no longer an option for me. I'm committed to pleasing God, and this journey has given me a deeper understanding of grace and favor. God has shown me that even though I didn't work to earn this, the gifts He placed inside me are what brought me here. Who He created me to be is enough for everything He's called me into—and the same applies to you. There will be occasions when what God is asking of you feels so much bigger than yourself, and it's tempting to run away. But know this: Even when you say no, God will lead you right back to where He wants you to be.

As I shared in my story, I told God no, but His unwavering faithfulness led me to the yes I was destined to give. Surrender is so much safer than running. It's time to stop running. No more denying the person God created you to be. No more shrinking back when your yes is leading you into spaces bigger than you ever imagined. No more letting the pain of your past create fear about your future. Trust God because, in the end, you will live in the fruit of your decisions—whether you choose to say yes or no.

Aligning with Yes

It's funny to think that by saying no we could escape an omnipresent God. As if He's not with us the entire time, pursuing us through everything. Nothing in the hands of God is ever wasted, including our nos. Sometimes our nos lead us to truer yeses, just like in Jonah's story.

I think we need to take a look at Jonah's life so we can understand that we can't run from God. The way He pursues us is relentless. God has a way of proving that He will continue to pursue us so we can serve the mission He created us for.

God commanded Jonah to take a message of judgment and deliverance to his enemies in Nineveh, the infamous Assyrians, but Jonah said no. He boarded a ship heading in the opposite direction. As a result, the ship was caught in a violent storm. Jonah's disobedience didn't just affect him—it endangered everyone aboard. Saying no to God placed Jonah outside His will and protection. When Jonah realized that his actions caused the storm, he told the crew to throw him overboard. To save them, Jonah had to die (Jonah 1:1–12).

There are four profound lessons here that lead to one major perspective shift. First, Jonah's story foreshadows Jesus. While death was our destiny, Jesus gave His life to save ours. Jonah serves as an early glimpse of that ultimate sacrifice. Second, it illustrates what it means to follow God's will: We must die to our own desires, expectations, and plans.

Third, God's will always prevails. After being thrown overboard, Jonah was swallowed by a huge fish. After Jonah prayed, God ordered the fish to spit him out on the beach. Then God once again called Jonah to Nineveh (1:17–2:10). It's a reminder that we can't run from God.

Fourth, running from God affects more than just us. Our decisions affect everyone connected to us—those within our immediate circle and those we were meant to influence with the love of Jesus. By stepping outside God's will, we hinder others from experiencing Him through us. Your life is about more than just you. Your choices have a ripple effect on the lives of others.

Now, listen closely. If Jonah had kept saying no, God could have just used someone else. God can raise up someone else. If you keep saying no, He will find another way to fulfill His plan, because His purpose always prevails. But God wants to use you. He wants you to say yes so He can develop the gifts He's given you.

So, let's shift the perspective. Instead of viewing God's calling as an attack on the life you want to live, see it as an invitation to partner with Him to advance His kingdom and carry out His mandate here on earth. Yes, it requires you to stop running, to lay down your life, and to put others ahead of yourself, but that's part of the journey.

Saying no to God is often rooted in forgetting that our lives don't belong to us. We've been entrusted with stewarding our lives according to His will. Even when an option outside God seems appealing, we must lean into His desires for us. I think of a camera my team uses when we're on the road. It's my camera, and because I'm familiar with it, they always come to me before using it. They could experiment with it, but the camera will function best when used in line with its design and under my guidance. The same is true for our lives. We often seek answers outside God about how to live our best lives, but He is our creator and knows what's best for us. No decision made outside His will can bring us greater fulfillment than one aligned with His plan.

The No That Leads to Yes

Sometimes the no we give to others is necessary so we can wholeheartedly surrender our yes to God. There have been countless times when I've had to turn down opportunities in order to stand firm in my commitment to Him. And sometimes choosing God's will means letting go of dreams we've held since childhood. Can you imagine letting go of a lifelong dream to say yes to the unknown? Our ability to make that choice boils down to how much we trust God.

Think about how we build trust in our natural relationships. One of my mentors, Pastor Rick, used to say, "Place trust in the gap." When you don't know someone well enough to utterly trust their character, you trust them until they prove otherwise. That same principle can apply to your relationship with God. If you're new to trusting Him or feel like you don't know Him well enough to surrender wholly, I encourage you to place trust in the gap.

In 2023, God was rapidly increasing my influence across all platforms, which naturally brought more exposure. One day, I received an email from a casting producer inviting me to be part of a reality show about pastors and dating set to air on a major network. It was like a childhood dream coming full circle. Growing up, I had always dreamed of being on TV and becoming a talk show host. While this wasn't my own talk show, it felt like an opportunity that aligned with that childhood desire, so I was sure it must be a God thing.

Sometimes our personal desires can cloud our judgment, making it hard to see the situation clearly. Here's a piece of advice: When you're trying to discern whether an opportunity is from God, submit it to prayer and consult a trusted voice. In my case, I invited my best friend to join me on the call with the casting producer so we could discuss afterward what we felt God was saying. The call was exciting, and I began to imagine the possibilities.

> *When you're trying to discern whether an opportunity is from God, submit it to prayer and consult a trusted voice.*

However, there were red flags. The biggest one was that, with reality TV, I wouldn't have control over how I was portrayed or how the final edit would come together. I told the producer I'd think about it and let him know my decision. Later, my best friend called and, without hesitation, said, "No." She pointed out that we could easily spiritualize it by saying the show would provide a bigger platform to share the gospel. But the truth was that being part of a reality show could tarnish my anointing. While an opportunity might seem good in the natural, if I were to step outside God's will by compromising, then I'd risk losing the authority and influence I was meant to carry.

Compromise diminishes your ability to influence the territory God has entrusted to you. When you compromise, you're essentially submitting your authority to whatever spirit or principality is at work in that space, which makes you ineffective in your role. So when an opportunity presents itself, you have to discern who it's from. Ask yourself, *Is this helping me point people to Jesus, or could it actually prevent me from doing that?*

Take the reality show, for example. If I were to submit to being part of one, the only thing I'd be able to control is myself, not the narrative or the environment. That lack of control doesn't sit well with me, because my calling is far too important and sacred to risk having it manipulated for entertainment.

Understanding this made me confident in my decision to turn it down. I also trusted the friend I consulted on the matter, which confirmed that I was making the right choice.

In the end, saying no to this opportunity was necessary to preserve my calling and stay aligned with God's purpose for my life. It was a reminder that not every open door is meant to be walked through—sometimes the no leads to a far greater yes.

Take an opportunity to think about this: What would have happened if Jesus had said yes to the temptations Satan offered instead of following God's plan (Luke 4:1–13)? Our lives and the world would be completely different. We must remember that every time we say yes to God, we contribute to building the kingdom of heaven. It expands His kingdom, allowing more people to encounter Jesus, while the kingdom of darkness loses ground. Our yes is powerful, and it makes a difference beyond just ourselves.

However, we also need to be mindful of the traps the enemy sets to tempt us to choose something over God. I often reflect on the times in my life when I was presented with opportunities that aligned with my desires but I knew they weren't from God. I had a responsibility to choose His path, especially because of the people who are affected by my ministry and influence. I may not always get it right, but as long as I remain surrendered and consult God, He keeps me on the right path.

I turned down that reality show, and a few months later, I ran into someone at a food tasting event. This person had attended Bible studies my friend and I used to host when I moved to L.A. in 2018. At this time, he was a supervising producer for a television network, and as we caught up, he mentioned how blessed he was by the growth of my ministry. Before he left, he offered me the chance to pitch my podcast for their network. I realized that my earlier decision to say no to the reality show had brought me to this new, God-ordained opportunity. I didn't have to chase it. It found me because I chose obedience.

What I love most about this is how God works. Our journey of saying yes to Him is built on trust. It's an ongoing relationship where, despite ups and downs, we choose to trust Him at every step.

Another Chance to Say Yes

We don't always make the right choice, though, like Moses when he struck the rock instead of speaking to it (Numbers 20:2–12). Regardless of our mess, God's purpose prevails.

Moses faced consequences, but God's will for the people was fulfilled. That story reminds me that, even in our disobedience, God's plan can still come to pass.

I've had times in my life when I said yes to something that ended up causing more harm than good, affecting not only me but also those around me. Yet God's grace provided a way out. There's a verse that says when temptation comes, God will always provide a way of escape:

> The temptations in your life are no different from what others experience. And God is faithful. He will not allow the temptation to be more than you can stand. When you are tempted, he will show you a way out so that you can endure. (1 Corinthians 10:13)

I've experienced firsthand God providing me ways of escape.

For example, there was a time I was online dating. I knew deep down that God had already told me to get off the dating apps, but I ignored Him. I had been listening to music filled with lust that fed my lonely spirit and planted seeds of temptation. Driven by that loneliness and impatience, I stepped into a real-life situation that almost led me down the wrong path.

In my disobedience, I met a guy I really liked who lived in San Diego. We had great conversations and even planned to attend a concert together. During the date, I clearly heard God say, "No" and "This is detrimental to your calling." I shrugged it off, enjoying our time together, but as the night went on, the warnings grew louder.

By the end of the evening, the conversation had veered into territory that was completely inappropriate for a first date, and it became clear that this man's intentions weren't aligned with mine. God had warned me, yet I had continued the date. It was a reminder of how easy it is to inch closer to disobedience when we ignore His voice. How dangerous it can be when we override God's direction. Thankfully, I walked away from the potentially compromising situation unscathed. God's mercy protected me from what could have been a harmful situation.

Even when we get it wrong, God's grace and mercy are still there to guide and protect us. Maybe you've said yes to God in words but not in actions, or maybe you've drifted from His will. I want to assure you that God isn't mad at you. He's still right where you left Him, waiting for you to return. He hasn't changed His mind about you, and He factored in every mistake you would make. His love for you remains the same, even in the mess-ups.

While there are consequences to our actions, God uses even those to grow us. He's not a distant, angry God punishing us for our mistakes. He's a loving Father who draws us closer to Himself through grace. Our relationship with Him isn't about being perfect; it's about progressing in our trust and obedience. So, if you've fallen short, don't be discouraged. Know that God's love for you is unwavering and He's giving you another chance to say yes.

The Freedom to Decline

Where there is an opportunity to say yes, saying no will always be an option. The hard truth is, wherever we can trace sin, we can trace a lack of trust in God. I can point to my own story as evidence. There were times I didn't want to say yes to God, because I was afraid and didn't trust His plans for me. Joining dating apps, for example, was my way of trying to take control of my future and the marriage I desire, essentially trying to make God fit into my timeline—as if He needed my help to fulfill His plans. The reality is, while God doesn't change His mind, He can change His methods. And sometimes that means raising up someone else to do what you won't.

One story from Scripture that stands out to me is Saul's. He was God's chosen king, but he allowed his fear of losing soldiers to guide his decisions. Instead of waiting for Samuel as God had instructed, Saul took matters into his own hands and offered the sacrifice himself. His disobedience cost him the throne; he forfeited the chance for his kingdom to be established forever. Because of that, God ended his reign and raised up someone else—David—to take his place (1 Samuel 13:7–14).

The lesson here is clear: Disobedience rooted in fear or mistrust can lead to forfeited blessings. When we choose our own ways over God's, we risk missing out on what He has for us. Trusting God means saying yes, even when it's uncomfortable, because the alternative may cost us more than we realize.

Disobedience rooted in fear or mistrust can lead to forfeited blessings.

Now, we can't transition away without also addressing the reasons we want to say no. I often find myself fearing that I'll step into something confidently but get it wrong. The sad truth is, that mindset keeps us from becoming all we need to be to embrace the moment.

I encourage you to reflect on what in you is making you want to say no. For Saul, it was fear and insecurity; he doubted his ability to lead the Israelites and felt unworthy of God's calling. Similarly, Moses initially said no out of a sense of inadequacy, believing he lacked the eloquence and courage to confront Pharaoh and lead the Israelites to freedom. For Jonah, it was his own prejudices; he didn't believe the people of Nineveh deserved God's mercy. But what he missed was that God's judgment was an act of mercy, a reflection of His compassion.

Sometimes our perspective on what God is calling us to do can prevent us from being the answer He's sending. Even how we see ourselves can block our yes. Let me be honest: When we're constantly weighing how something will make us feel or what we'll lose against what God is asking us to do, we may have an issue with pride. Those concerns are self-focused. Our nos focus on our fears and inadequacies, rather than the potential God has placed within us to affect the world around us.

I want to challenge you to dig deep and examine the root of those fears. You don't have to worry about not being enough when God is the one calling you, because He's a God who doesn't lie and never fails. If He's within you, guiding you to take a step toward His instruction, know that you won't fail.

My dad used to say, "Nothing beats a failure but a try." I didn't understand it at the time, but now I realize that the only way we can truly fail is if we never try. The only way we lose is if we never step into the opportunity, if we let the enemy's lies keep us from saying yes to God.

Pause + Reflect

My prayer is that you recognize your freedom to say no yet still feel compelled to say yes along your journey. Saying yes opens the door to incredible possibilities and aligns us with God's desires for our lives. When we completely embrace the love of God and trust in His plans, saying yes becomes a natural response to His call. Conversely, saying no may seem safe, but it can lead to missed opportunities and a distancing from the fulfillment He desires for us. I sometimes feel unworthy, and that feeling isn't wrong—I don't deserve God's love. But He gives it freely. He loved me enough to choose me, and He loves you enough to choose you. Once we embrace love fully, choosing Him becomes one of the easiest and most fulfilling journeys we'll ever take.

1. What opportunities might open in your life if you choose to say yes to God instead of hesitating?

2. What fears or insecurities are leading you to say no to God's calling on your life, and how are they holding you back?

3. Are you allowing pride or self-centered thinking to overshadow the impact God wants to make through you? If so, how can you surrender those patterns of thought to Him?

4. How does trusting in the character of God—His faithfulness, omnipresence, and love—give you confidence to say yes, even when you feel uncertain or unworthy?

9

Does the Journey Ever End?

Father, if you are willing, please take this cup of suffering away from me. Yet I want your will to be done, not mine.
—Luke 22:42

I said yes to the Lord when I was just six years old. At that time, I thought all it took was to declare, "Yes, I want to accept Jesus as my Lord and Savior." I remember the long walk down the aisle and sitting in front of the entire congregation at Mount Olive Missionary Baptist Church, where my journey of yes began.

I wish I could say that the yes I gave back then has carried me through to today, but it hasn't. Instead, I've come to realize that the journey of yes is ongoing. It's a continuous pursuit of Jesus. It mirrors the passionate journey of the woman with the issue of blood, the mistakes of David followed by his cries for forgiveness, and Peter's denial of Christ followed by his restoration and calling to build the church. The journey of yes never truly ends. If we lose sight of this truth, then we can become frustrated.

The journey of yes never truly ends.

There have been instances in my life when I questioned whether I would reach a point where I wouldn't have to keep sacrificing or laying things down. I wondered, *Does this ever come to an end?* Those questions sometimes stem from a place of exhaustion, yet I find comfort in knowing that even my Savior faced hesitation, asking if there might be someone else to take on the task. I recall times when I prayed honestly, saying, "God, I don't want to do this anymore. I think You should find someone else—not because I feel unqualified, but because of the pressure it puts on our relationship."

One of the riskiest years I've experienced was 2023. I was navigating a faith journey regarding my life, career, and purpose while choosing to believe in God despite the challenges I was facing. In January, as I chose to trust God and leave my job for a more uncertain path, my dad was diagnosed with prostate cancer—a devastating blow that shook my faith.

I wanted to be the strong one for my parents, to proclaim faith even when my own belief wavered. Yet I struggled to cling to God's promises because my past disappointments had resurfaced in my heart. Having lost my grandfather to the same illness during college, I had already walked a similar path. His death weighed heavily on me. For the first time in my life, I feared that my dad might die, and nothing had ever gripped my heart in that way before.

When we realize we're facing a trial or spiritual attack, we often rally in prayer and bold faith, ready to fight back. But I immediately detached my emotions from the situation; I wasn't talking about it or crying. I was numb. Afraid to confront my emotions, fearing that doing so would overwhelm me.

I hid behind platitudes like "God is in control" or "I just have to believe." Yet even as I recited those phrases, they did little to quell the growing fear in my heart that my dad could die. My fear paralyzed my faith; I stopped praying about the situation, afraid to believe only to face disappointment if my dad didn't survive.

One morning, I was on the phone with my best friend, who was praying for me concerning my dad. I was reciting the typical Christian reassurances about believing for healing when she interrupted me: "Brenda, how do you really feel?"

In vulnerability, I admitted, "I am scared. What if my dad dies and never gets to walk me down the aisle or bond with my children?"

Her question created space for me to be honest. I thought that avoiding my feelings was the safer choice. I could manage the situation no matter the outcome. But the more I ran from my feelings and God, the more lost I became. I didn't know how to process any of it. I found myself wondering, *Does this journey ever end? Will I always be fighting the odds? Can the good times last just a little longer?*

I think I began wondering about an end to this journey because I had just walked away from everything that felt stable. On one side, I was trusting that God was leading me exactly where I needed to be. On the other side, I was contending for my father's healing. The journey was heavy, and I was tired. I wanted it to be over.

I had to say yes to trusting God, no matter what that trust might bring. This was one of the hardest yeses to give; it required more than just words—it demanded a deep acceptance in my heart. I understood that life comes with trials and that we should "count it all joy" (James 1:2, ESV). I knew that trials build endurance (verse 3)—and in hindsight, I can see that clearly. But that diagnosis hit me hard. I felt forsaken by the God I was dedicating my life to. It can be difficult to accept His presence when the outcome doesn't match our desires, but just because He shows up in ways we don't expect doesn't mean He hasn't shown up.

Looking back, I appreciate God's wisdom in allowing these two journeys to align. By walking away from my full-time job in California, I gained the flexibility to be present with my parents during that season. I was able to fly in for doctor's appointments and be there for them in ways I couldn't have been if I had remained tied to my job. We were blessed to share meaningful prayer and quality time. Throughout it all, I can clearly see God's intentionality. Saying yes to this season wasn't just a leap of faith—it was God guiding me to where I needed to be.

The Never-Ending Journey

In August 2023, my dad had surgery while I was on a plane, heading to Canada to preach. I remember waiting at LAX for my flight, overcome with guilt, thinking, *I should be by his side*. As I stood in line at Starbucks, my assistant sent me a voice note that completely unraveled me. I listened to her words and just started crying, feeling deeply encouraged by the Lord. She said simply, "Brenda, God has never failed you, and He won't fail you now." It was the reminder I needed— that, whenever I've needed Him, God has always shown up. Even in times when I wanted to go my own way, He was there. I broke down in line because God met me right where I was and spoke to the fears in my heart that I had never uttered. That's what gave me the full trust and capacity to say yes to His call for me to preach, even when my heart wanted to be with my dad.

Every time we surrender, we tend to focus on what we might lose. We get caught up in the transitions and lifestyle changes and miss out on the true gift of obedience. As we've seen, the journey of yes isn't really about the yes itself—it's about the God we discover along the way. Each time we say yes to Him, we're given the opportunity to experience a new layer of His character. That's what makes the journey of yes never ending. We could live a thousand lifetimes and never entirely discover the depths of who God is. I would have never known God as a healer if I hadn't experienced Him healing my dad.

We could live a thousand lifetimes and never entirely discover the depths of who God is.

When I boarded that plane, I didn't know what to expect. But before I even reached my connecting flight, my dad was already out of surgery, cracking jokes thanks to the anesthesia. I remember the relief of hearing his voice. He told me, "Brenda, I'm proud of you. The best way you could have honored me was by trusting God, staying on assignment, and serving the Lord."

While I'm on the road doing the Father's work—preaching the gospel and walking in my purpose—God is taking care of everything else. My life verse, Matthew 6:33, which you will hear me quote all the time, is lived out during this season:

> Seek the Kingdom of God above all else, and live righteously, and he will give you everything you need.

After my dad had his prostate removed, he was declared cancer-free, and we thought that chapter was over. But in July 2024, we faced another scare. A doctor told us that the cancer had spread and that my dad would need chemotherapy. I remember telling my mom that we should get a second opinion. We prayed, and it turned out to be a misdiagnosis. Even though my dad remains cancer-free, it has been a continuous journey of faith to believe that he is truly healed and will stay that way.

Persevere in the Journey

Our journeys have so many layers, and with each yes, we take a step deeper into intimacy with our Father. But when we hit what feel like lows, it's easy to wonder, *Will this ever end?*

Sometimes the pressure is so overwhelming that we just want to give up.

I grew up playing sports and was involved in extracurricular activities. Whenever something didn't go my way or felt harder than I had expected, my instinct was always to quit and try something else. But my parents wouldn't allow it. Even now as an adult, I can still hear them saying what they told me as a child: "We don't quit; we finish."

I want to offer you that same advice—don't quit; finish. In a time when soft parenting is more common, this advice might seem a little harsh, but for me, it took the pressure off. My parents weren't asking me to be perfect or to be the best at everything. They just wanted me to put forth the effort and see things through to the end. Even if I didn't come out on top, I learned valuable lessons and grew by completing what I started. Life is the same way. You don't have to succeed in every opportunity, but the only way to reach the outcome God intends is to finish.

The most amazing part of saying yes is that we never have to finish alone. God is Immanuel—God with us.

We aren't alone in the hard things that often push us to ask God to relieve us from the journey. Earlier I mentioned the defining point Jesus has when He expresses, *I really don't want to do this, God, so if You want to change Your mind, now would be the time.* Just like Jesus in the Garden of Gethsemane, we will have moments when we will ask God to let a yes pass us by. And we usually want it to pass us by because we don't want it to separate us from our desires and our plan—the way we thought things were going to turn out. Sometimes we are avoiding the yes because we are looking for an escape from the pruning seasons that are so difficult.

There is a difference between our avoidance and the garden experience, though. Jesus's hesitance was a response to being separated, for the first time in His life, from the presence of His Father. We read this story to highlight when Jesus expressed that He didn't want to do what God wanted Him to do. True, but His reasoning was quite different from our usually selfish one. Our Savior completely understands the feelings we have—Jesus has felt everything that we feel. But His longing for the presence of God should inspire our obedience, not our disobedience.

In the garden, Jesus was sitting face-to-face with an invitation to die. To sacrifice Himself so that we could have the freedom to choose to follow in His footsteps. To die for God's sake—for His purpose, for His plan, for His will. To die to Himself so that others could encounter Him and experience a life of righteousness and the gift of eternal life. Faced with death, Jesus still ended that with "Not my will, but yours be done" (Luke 22:42, NIV). And that is how we persevere in the never-ending journey. As we work out our obedient response to God, we say, "God, I don't want to do this, but ultimately let me settle into Your will. Not mine, but Yours be done."

I wish I could say I've mastered the journey of saying yes, but the reality is that the Lord has continually brought me face-to-face with those "not my will, but His will be done" moments. They often present themselves as enticing doors of compromise. My unique calling finds me at the intersection of faith and culture, both in my ministry and in my personal life.

As a minister, I need to be intentional about the places I go and the people I engage with, ensuring that I authentically represent Christ wherever I am. Also, I must be sure that the intention behind my yes is always to bring God glory. Satan isn't always overt in his temptations; he is cunning and deceptive. He identifies the hidden desires in my heart—those things I may not even recognize—and uses them against me.

After leaving my job at Centerpoint, I was presented with all these other opportunities that were seemingly blessings—ways toward financial security. There was always an opportunity to step outside the will of God. I can't tell you how many times my friends would offer me opportunities, but I would never have peace to move forward. I found myself so frustrated with not having answers to the questions and suggestions from my community. During that time, though, God was working out of my heart the things that would hinder my next season. The process was necessary.

Listen, my family and friends love me deeply. That helps me understand that all the questions and suggestions they offer during the journey should never be taken as them being against me. They just want what is best for me. But the enemy was using those close to me and their love for me to exploit a hidden desire in my heart: financial stability. In reality, this was a distraction meant to detour the destiny that God had designed for me.

God wanted me to experience His provision. The way He provided in the Bible is the same way He can provide today. The God who made fresh manna fall from heaven every morning to feed the Israelites and who sent Elijah to a brook to be fed every day is the same God who provided for me for an entire year without a full-time job and without any plans. Even now, I've never had to post that I'm available for booking, yet I find my calendar full of speaking engagements and invitations to be a part of things. The God of the Bible is the same God who looks out for me. To discover this truth, though, I had to say, "Not my will, Lord, but Yours be done."

When your life is surrendered to the will of God, you can end up smack dab in the middle of a blessing you didn't dream of, far above anything you ever imagined.

I always like to say that my yes gave God something to breathe on. When your life is surrendered to the will of God, you can end up smack dab in the middle of a blessing you didn't dream of, far above anything you ever imagined. I'm amazed at how much the Lord really did have this thing planned out. His promise rings truer and fuels my perseverance:

"I know the plans I have for you," says the LORD. "They are plans for good and not for disaster, to give you a future and a hope." (Jeremiah 29:11)

Build Faith for the Long Haul

In Jeremiah 29:11, the Lord was talking to a people in a season of exile. I felt that way. I felt like the Lord had me walk away from every source of income, every piece of stability I had. He removed those things, all the while saying, "I have plans to prosper you." It was evident. It was my last day on my job being February 8 and my first assignment on the road being February 17—just nine days later. That's not coincidence. That's not happenstance. That's the plans and purposes of God working out as I took steps. But with that came the enemy with a subtle invitation to compromise.

In April 2023, I had just hosted my first pop-up Bible study in Atlanta and went out to eat with a few friends. One of them, who's like a little brother to me and an absolute genius in creative marketing, started brainstorming ways I could maintain financial stability while waiting for God to reveal my next steps—there's that hidden desire of my heart showing up again.

As we discussed platforms like TikTok, he said, "You should do motivational videos, but maybe dial down the Jesus talk. Make it more faith-based but without explicitly mentioning Jesus. That way, it'll be more palatable for a broader audience. You could reach people who aren't specifically looking for faith-based content. And once you're in the room, then—bam—you hit them with the faith."

To be completely honest, what he was saying made a lot of sense. It sounded like solid advice. Coming from a background in creative marketing and content creation, I knew that these strategies could open doors and create opportunities. But as good as his advice was, it didn't sit right with me.

In seasons of uncertainty, there's often pressure to figure things out and come up with plans when we don't thoroughly understand what God is doing. We might be tempted to detour from His path to find stability or explanations. But sometimes we must be comfortable with saying, "I don't know." We have to say yes again, not just to God's plans, but also to navigating the unknown without clear answers.

That entire season of my life taught me how to trust God, even when I couldn't explain things to others. My parents were constantly calling, asking what God was saying, what my plan was, and how I would manage without a job or a place to stay. But despite the fact that I didn't have all the answers, God provided for me every step of the way. I had to be okay with the uncertainty, knowing that He was directing each step.

Some journeys of saying yes are not about what we gain but about who we become. For a long time, I didn't see fruit, but my faith was being built. Every time I needed something, God showed up. Every time I chose to remain faithful to what He told me and ignored the noise from others who thought I should take a different path, God moved.

That night, I wrestled with the idea, wondering if this could be God's way of providing financial stability while His bigger plans unfolded. But in prayer, He gave me Mark 8:36: "What does it profit a man to gain the whole world and forfeit his soul?" (ESV).

At this point, I understood a few things. First, if I pursued those opportunities, they would come at a greater cost—

denying Jesus in my content to make it more acceptable wasn't an option. God was asking me, "What does it profit you to gain more followers, influence, or opportunities if it means losing your soul?" The entire point of this life is to draw people to Jesus, and what we do for Him will outlast anything else when we leave this world.

> *The entire point of this life is to draw people to Jesus, and what we do for Him will outlast anything else when we leave this world.*

I also understood more clearly who I truly am. I'm not a faith-based content creator—I'm a content creator whose life is rooted in faith. I can't create anything without including God, because He's a part of every aspect of my life. Where I work, where I live, and how I move are all influenced by Jesus. To create content without Him would be a betrayal of my true self.

We must be clear about what God is calling us to do, because our journeys are different. I realized that even if no one else understood, I had to be confident in the path God set for me. That conversation helped me see the importance of protecting my journey and not sharing everything with everyone. Some things people just must watch unfold.

The Little Things

The journey doesn't end. Sometimes it continues in huge decisions, like walking away from a job or turning down an opportunity that aligns with childhood dreams. And sometimes it continues in those little decisions, like turning off the secular music or keeping what you watch on TV in check. The little things are important. They build your character and develop you to be Christlike.

I'm often challenged in the little yeses that highlight this never-ending journey. I usually have the misconception that because I told God yes in the big things, I will be set for a few months or a year. But one little yes that regularly comes up is taking adequate time to rest. There was a particular season in my life when every few months God was challenging me to walk away from the busyness of my life and rest.

I found myself in a season when I was juggling everything—podcasting, preaching, traveling every week, studying in seminary, working on creative projects, and trying to expand my influence beyond the faith-based space. I even decided to take my pop-up Bible studies on a tour.

But then I reached a crossroads. I realized I was doing all of this *for* God but on the edge of burnout. It felt like He was saying, "Could you pause and just be with Me as your God?" As I considered His question, I saw the imbalance—there was far more output than input. I was pouring out constantly yet hardly being poured into. God recognized I needed Him more than I needed to be a vessel for Him. I was so focused on showing up for all my commitments and roles that I neglected the rest my soul desperately needed.

Rest isn't always about sleep. It's also about working from a place of peace, knowing God is in control. I came to see that I hadn't been operating from that place. When God asked me to pause, it wasn't easy. My mind raced with thoughts about all the commitments I'd made, the people who needed what I was offering, and having to explain why I was taking a breather. A lot of my resistance was driven by ego. I'd announced plans, and the thought of going back and saying, "Actually, we're not doing this," was tough. But I felt God gently saying, "Either you trust Me or you don't."

Could I trust Him enough to walk away, even when everything I'd been working for seemed to be happening? Could I trust Him enough to take a break from the work that sustained me, believing that He would sustain me even more? I had to remind myself, *The God who gave me these opportunities is more than capable of holding them while He asks me to pause.*

So, I hit pause—not stop, not quit, but pause. I couldn't keep running when my tank was on empty. God was inviting me to allow Him to fill me because I had reached a point of depletion. I paused long enough to see the areas in my heart that were hidden by busyness. And in the stillness, I realized I wasn't okay. I was definitely having a Psalm 23 encounter. God was making me lie down in green pastures and leading me beside still waters (verse 2).

I love how God challenges me in this way. Often we think He's trying to take things away from us when, in reality, He's trying to ensure that we fulfill the very purpose He created us for. At the rate I was going, I wouldn't have had the longevity needed for the calling on my life. I had to step back, trust God to take care of me, and allow Him to lead me through that pause.

I shut everything down. I got off social media, postponed the tour, and stopped traveling for thirty days. I focused on seminary, went back to therapy, and found a church where I could simply sit and be poured into—where no one knew me and I could receive the Word like anyone else. That season was everything I didn't know I needed.

God used my friends, my family, and my community to pour back into me. I'd get text messages that spoke directly to things He had already whispered, providing clarity and confirmation. He began to refine me, putting the pieces back together so I could be the person capable of carrying out the calling He placed on my life.

I think about John 15, where it talks about bearing fruit—how even when a branch is bearing good fruit, it still needs pruning (verse 2). Even when things are going well, God will cut away anything that might hinder future growth. That season was a pruning for me. I realized that my role in other people's lives wasn't to be their savior—I was simply a vessel. When God partners with us to affect the lives of others and we experience the fruit of that, sometimes we think it's our responsibility to always be available and accessible. It could just be me, but sometimes we can lose sight that God chooses to invite us into assignments. Just as He used me, He could raise up others while I took this step of obedience.

And in that pause, I rediscovered my love for the Word and my relationship with Jesus. It reminds me of Revelation 2:3–4, where Jesus said to the church, "You've persevered, but you've forgotten your first love." Sometimes, as ministers or servants of the kingdom, we think our worth is tied to how much we do for God. But the truth is, God cares more about being with us than what we do for Him.

While I was doing all the right things, I had lost sight of my first love—Jesus. I do what I do because of Him. Everything I do should be an overflow of my intimate relationship with Jesus, not just a commitment I check off.

God reminded me that, without the influence, the followers, the speaking engagements, the podcast—without all of that—it's just me and Him. And that's all it ever needs to be. When all is said and done, when this life fades, the only thing that remains is my relationship with Jesus. That's what matters most, and that's what I have to work the hardest to sustain.

So, if you're wondering whether this journey ever ends, the answer is no. The journey of yes is a never-ending adventure into deeper intimacy with Jesus. And that deep relationship with Him is what gives us the courage and strength to say yes to whatever He asks next.

Pause + Reflect

Now, here is your chance to respond. Before you can totally trust God, you must identify what's in your heart that keeps you from choosing His will over your own. This is the time to be honest with God and ask, "Search my heart, and reveal what makes me want to walk away from You." Ask Him to show you the things you've been holding on to, perhaps even loving more than Him. It's easy to think that only tangible things distract us, but when I reflect on the time my dad was diagnosed with cancer, I realize I could have chosen anger toward God. I could have said, "I've sacrificed so much for You—why would You allow my dad to go through this?" It would have been easy to choose my emotions over my faith. It was incredibly difficult to trust God while navigating the biggest faith move of my life and at the same time dealing with my dad's diagnosis.

Surrender is not just about letting go of material things but also about releasing our attachment to outcomes and our sense of entitlement. We were never promised a life without trials. We live in a fallen world, and while the kingdom of God is both present and coming, we are not yet living in its fullness. So, we must reach the place where we can say, "Even if the outcome isn't what I desire, God, not my will, but Yours be done." It's a powerful statement, but when it takes root in your heart, nothing will shake your faith. You'll recognize that God is sovereign, and when explanations elude you, you can trust in His sovereignty.

1. What are the hidden desires or attachments in your heart that might be keeping you from completely surrendering to God's will?

2. How do you respond when God's plan or the outcomes in your life don't align with your desires, and how does this affect your trust in His sovereignty?

3. Have you ever found yourself placing more trust in outcomes than in God Himself? How can you shift your focus from the result to God's greater plan?

4. In times of difficulty, how can you practice saying, "Not my will, but Yours be done," and what might this look like in your current situation?

Conclusion

The Ultimate Yes

I consider everything a loss because of the surpassing worth of knowing Christ Jesus my Lord, for whose sake I have lost all things. I consider them garbage, that I may gain Christ and be found in him, not having a righteousness of my own that comes from the law, but that which is through faith in Christ—the righteousness that comes from God on the basis of faith.

—Philippians 3:8–9, NIV

During my journey of saying yes to God, the biggest shift in my thinking came when I realized that He was impressed not by how much I could do for Him but by my willingness to walk with Him. For a long time, I believed that success in my walk with God was defined by my efforts and obedience. When I started seminary, I was anxious because I didn't want my growing knowledge of God to interfere with my intimacy with Him. In my first week of class, I voiced this fear, and the best advice I received was simple: "Take this journey with God."

That advice became the foundation for my understanding of the journey of yes. It's not about proving to God that you're worthy or about how many opportunities you seize to reflect His glory. Whether you're on a stage, in a classroom, or working a regular job, the true reward isn't the spotlight—it's the privilege of walking with God every day. The beauty of saying yes lies in the fellowship we have with Him.

> *The beauty of saying yes lies in the fellowship we have with Him.*

Recently, I was preaching on Ephesians 2:1–10, and it wrecked me. Paul wrote about the depth of God's grace and love, reminding us that even though we were dead in our sins, God, in His mercy, made us alive in Christ. Not because of our works, but because of His grace. As I read this passage, I was reminded that our obedience is not about earning God's favor but about responding to the grace He's already given us.

When we embrace the magnitude of the gift that God gave us in Christ Jesus, our yes is all we have to give. It doesn't earn us anything, but it postures us to do the works that God prepared for us to do. When the gift is received, we become enough to handle the assignment. We have the Holy Spirit leading and guiding us along the way. When we say yes to God, we're stepping into the purpose He's had for us all along.

I think of a song I grew up listening to: "Will your heart and soul say yes?"* That simple question continues to echo in my mind. God asks us if we will say yes to Him, and every yes draws us closer to the person He created us to be. But here's

---

* "Yes," track 27 on Shekinah Glory Ministry, *Live,* Kingdom Records, 2004.

the thing: Our yes is more than just obedience. It's surrender. We relinquish control, trusting that God's plans far exceed our own. When we hold the reins of our lives, our vision is limited to what we can conceive. But when we surrender to God, the possibilities become endless. As Ephesians 3:20 says, He can do "exceedingly abundantly above all that we ask or think" (NKJV).

Saying yes to God means declaring, "I desire all that You have for me, even if it requires sacrificing my own desires." This can be a challenging choice, yet it brings eternal rewards. As I reflect on saying yes to God—especially during times of reluctance—I realize that each yes was invaluable. It was not about what I gained but about who I became through the experience. My willingness to say yes has transformed me, deepened my relationship with Him, and affected those around me and even strangers across the globe.

There's a story that beautifully illustrates the ripple effect of obedience. Imagine Mary, a young girl, being visited by an angel and asked to carry the Son of God. Her yes came at a great cost. She risked being ostracized by her culture, nearly lost her fiancé, and faced lifelong whispers about her son's legitimacy. She watched as her son grew up, faced rejection, died a brutal death, and then disappeared into the tomb. Yet her yes—the yes that came with heartache and sacrifice—changed the course of history. Through her obedience, salvation was made possible for the entire world.

Mary's yes didn't make sense at the time. It came with great pain, but the ripple effect was incomprehensible. And just as her yes paved the way for the salvation of the world, so our yeses can have a lasting impact that we may never see or understand in this lifetime. What might it look like if we truly believed that each of our small yeses could ripple out in ways we can't even imagine?

It reminds me of Peter's story in Luke 5. He had been fishing all night with no success and was ready to give up. But when Jesus asked to use his boat, Peter said yes. After preaching, Jesus told Peter to cast his nets again. Despite his exhaustion and doubt, Peter obeyed, and his nets were filled with so many fish that they couldn't contain them all. But here's the part that gets me: Peter didn't stay with the fish. Instead of basking in his sudden success, he left it all behind to follow Jesus. His yes wasn't about the immediate gain; it was about following the One who had called him.

The journey of yes is like that—sometimes we experience blessings beyond what we could have imagined, but the true reward is found in following Jesus. Our yeses may bring abundance, but the real treasure is intimacy with God.

So, I leave you with this question: *Will your heart and soul say yes?* Yes to a lifetime of surrender, yes to walking with God even when it costs you. I promise you, it's worth it—not because of the things you'll gain, but because of the transformation that will happen in you. You'll become the person God created you to be. And as you grow closer to Him, you'll discover that the greatest gift is not the things we receive but the One we walk with.

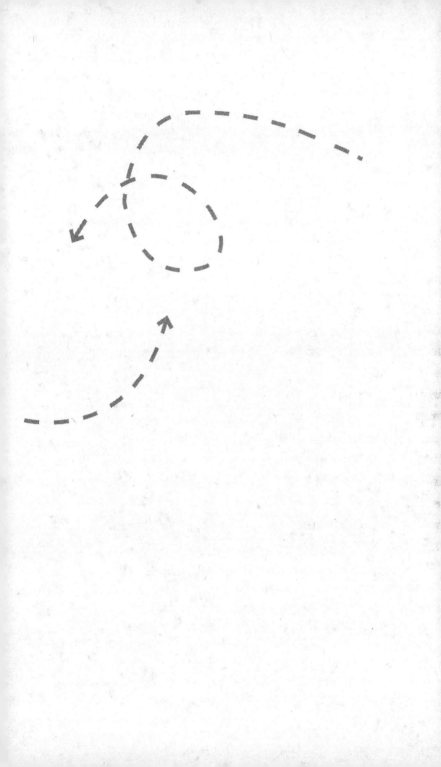

Acknowledgments

First and foremost, I give honor to God, who is the head of my life and the One who entrusted me with the assignment of writing *The Journey of Yes*. Never in my wildest dreams did I imagine that stepping out of the boat and following You into the unknown would lead to me becoming an author. Thank You, Lord, for trusting me with the gift of guiding others toward You!

This journey has been one of the most transformative experiences of my life. Incredible people have walked beside me every step, through every challenge and breakthrough. I'm blessed to have a village of family, friends, and other supporters who have encouraged, prayed for, and stood with me. This book is a testament to the power of community, and I'm beyond thankful for everyone who helped make it a reality. Here are just a few of the many people I want to acknowledge.

Mommy and **Daddy**—this entire book is dedicated to you, but I also want to take an opportunity to thank you for being my lifelong supporters. From day one, you've been my champions, my financiers, and my constant source of encouragement. You both are Team "How do we make this happen?"—always!

Your faith in me has been the foundation for everything, and I'm forever grateful.

Stephie, my sister—no one could ever know me like you do. You've been part of every story in this book, somehow involved in every chapter of my life. God knew what He was doing when He gave us to each other. I wouldn't want to run this race with anyone else. Thank you for everything, and a huge shout-out to your amazing husband, **Ifeayni**, and my precious niece (aka my rich bestie), **Ari**, for being my L.A. family. Love you all so deeply!

ONE L.A., the church that restored my life—where would I be if I hadn't stepped through your doors on May 20, 2018? My spiritual parents, **Pastor Touré** and **Pastor Sarah Jakes Roberts**—thank you for your yes that I get to live in the fruit of your guidance and your belief in me. Even before I knew all that I carried, you both saw it and called it out. I'm honored to be under your leadership.

My Centerpoint family, where I began preaching—thank you for your love and support. **Pastor John** and **Pastor Ann Hansen**—you have some of the purest hearts, and I'll always be thankful for the opportunities you gave me to grow and serve. The fruit of this book is rooted in my time at Centerpoint. To the entire staff and congregation—Centerpoint will forever be home. Love y'all so much!

Nik, my bestie—God used you in ways I could have never expected. We've weathered some dark times together, but God gave us each other to help us endure. So many of the times I said yes were journeys we got to share. I'm forever grateful for that time when you knocked on my door relentlessly, making sure I lived to write this book. We're locked in for life, Nik. Love you!

Randy, my brother—I can only describe you as selfless. When I moved to L.A., you didn't hesitate to welcome me, even in my brokenness. You gave me a space to heal, a place to pick up the shattered pieces of my heart and life. My journey is marked by your kindness! Thank you for helping me get back on my feet. I got you for life! Love you!

Brunes, my best friend and brother—I'll never forget your generosity during one of the biggest journeys I've ever taken. The book made it out of the group chat. Your friendship has been a lifeline, and your constant push for me to be better has meant everything. I'm so grateful to have you in my corner.

Team BP—Antwan, **Emma**, **Ashlee**, **Bri** (my mini-me), and **Tay**—y'all are the beat to my heart, the engine that keeps this machine running. We had no idea what we were building, but here we are. You travel with me, run podcasts, answer emails, listen to all my crazy ideas, and work miracles with no budget. You are a vital part of the vision God has given me. There is no BP without Team BP, and I'm deeply grateful for your sacrifice, dedication, and belief in me. We're pushing the kingdom forward together!

Tay, aka my human notepad—you've been my ride-or-die through everything. From traveling with me to helping me process ideas, you've been a vault for all my thoughts and struggles. You've heard me read chapters over and over, picked out my wardrobe, and reminded me not to wear Nike socks with everything. Words can't express my gratitude for the gift God gave me in you. Love you so much, little sis.

Acknowledgments

My girls, the ones who've held me down through life. **B-Low**, **Bry**, **Bree**, and **Tryce**, my lifelong best friends—I love you all deeply. From college to marriages, babies, breakups, and major achievements, we've been together for fifteen years, and I know God has more in store for us. Thank you for always riding with me and loving me for who I am.

My other girlies + my tribe, the ones who've held me accountable throughout this book-writing process, whether through texts, phone calls, or other check-ins—you've all played a role in getting me across the finish line. This book is as much yours as it is mine. I'm forever grateful that we get to do life together.

The entire WaterBrook team—thank you for embarking on this journey and believing in me and the vision. This book wouldn't have happened without you. **Luverta Reames**—thank you for your persistence and for seeing the story I needed to tell. **Estee Zandee**—thank you for your patience and for pushing me to be a better writer. **Kim Von Fange**, thank you for hopping into this process and never missing a beat. I was smitten by your genius and the way you understood my writing style out the gate! You are a GOAT!

Andrea, my literary agent—thank you for holding it down and navigating this new space for me. I've learned so much from you.

Jonny, you crafted a cover that beautifully captures both the heart of my book and my creative spirit. Thank you for your patience throughout the process and for sharing your incredible talent with this project!

My *Life in Perspective* audience, my family—you've been with me since the beginning, from my studio apartment in Long Beach to now. Thank you for pulling out of me what God placed in me for you. I'm honored to serve you.

My big family, including my siblings (I'm graced to be the youngest of ten!)—thank you for shaping me into the woman I am today.

This book is for you all. Onward and upward with God. Peace!

© RICARDO HUMES

BRENDA PALMER is an author, preacher, and podcaster. Born in Chicago, she discovered her passion for making a difference early on, leading her to earn degrees from Mississippi Valley State University and Syracuse University. She is currently pursuing a master of arts in biblical and theological studies at Denver Seminary.

Whether she is creating content, leading Bible studies, or hosting her podcast, Brenda has dedicated her life to preaching the gospel and ensuring others experience authentic encounters with Jesus. As the leader of Come Alive Collective, a movement offering nationwide Bible studies and worship nights, Brenda believes life unfolds through surrendering to God's plan. Her podcast, *Life in Perspective,* explores personal growth and self-discovery, resonating deeply with listeners through thought-provoking conversations and inspiring stories.

Brenda's authenticity and faith-driven approach make her a beacon of hope for many. With a growing social following, she leverages her influence to inspire change and foster a world where faith and creativity intersect seamlessly.

About the Type

This book was set in Cheltenham, a typeface created in 1896 by a distinguished American architect, Bertram Grosvenor Goodhue (1869–1924), and produced at the Cheltenham Press in New York in 1902 by Ingalls Kimball, who suggested that the face be called Cheltenham. It was designed with long ascenders and short descenders as a result of legibility studies indicating that the eye identifies letters by scanning their tops. The Mergenthaler Linotype Company put the typeface on machine in 1906, and Cheltenham has maintained its popularity for more than a century.